The
Uninvited
Goddess

Awakening to a New Era

Judith Perry Carpenter

The Uninvited Goddess: Awakening to a New Era
Copyright © 2019 Judith Perry Carpenter

ISBN: 978-1-63381-195-9

The cover photo, Jekyll Island MW1, was taken by my nephew, Jason Perry. It comes from his series of photographs called "The Night Sky," which focuses on the Milky Way, the Aurora, and star trails. I am honored and deeply grateful that he agreed to let me use this powerful image as my book cover.

Designed and produced by:
Maine Authors Publishing
12 High Street, Thomaston, Maine
www.maineauthorspublishing.com

Printed in the United States of America

To Jack, the love of my life and my companion on the journey,
to our wise and loving children,
and to our beautiful and gifted granddaughters
and all others born in the Era of Eris:
may you become wise and compassionate servants
of peace and justice in our troubled world.

Table of Contents

The other face of our pain for the world
is our love for the world,
our absolutely inseparable connectedness with all life.

—Joanna Macy

Let's remake the world with words.
Not frivolously, nor
To hide from what we fear,
But with a purpose.

—Gregory Orr

Tell me, what is it you plan to do
With your one wild and precious life?

—Mary Oliver, "The Summer Day"

Prologue

Like many of us, I have had a life full of awakenings, and, like most of us, I have lived a life I could not have foreseen. My journey led me to create a mixed-race family, become an Episcopal priest, work primarily with young girls and women, study feminist liberation theology and ministry, and avidly explore such things as Buddhist meditation, astrology, the Enneagram, and anything I can understand of quantum theory and consciousness. I am passionate about justice, inclusion, and the health of our planet, so, again like many, I find the polarization and toxicity of these times very disturbing. I have also become captivated by an archetype, Eris, which is the name of our newest planet. All of these stories are woven into this book.

I begin with Eris. In January 2005, a small and very distant body orbiting our sun was discovered by a Palomar Observatory team of astronomers from the California Institute of Technology. Believing it to be the long-sought planet X, the tenth planet, the team leader, Dr. Michael E. Brown, nicknamed it Xena, after the justice-seeking warrior princess of TV fame. This discovery proved disruptive within the official International Astronomical Union (IAU), whose job it is to categorize such bodies. The category of *planet* was reserved for the largest and most significant orbiting bodies, so apparently Pluto's designation as a planet had always been somewhat in dispute because of its small size. Therefore the officials were reluctant to accord Xena, slightly larger, planetary status, too. Maybe a new category was needed since there would undoubtedly be many more such bodies discovered, given technology's increasing ability to search the farthest reaches of the solar system. Finally, in August 2006, Xena was officially recognized and designated a *dwarf planet* by the IAU. Their description of a dwarf planet demoted Pluto to that category and elevated Ceres, the largest of the asteroids, to the same category. Due to the controversy surrounding this decision and the resulting uproar from devotees of Pluto, Dr. Brown requested that his Xena officially be named Eris after the relatively unknown Greek goddess of strife and discord, whose actions led to similarly troublesome arguments. Because he was lead discoverer, his choice carried the day.

Eris was the goddess who showed up uninvited at a wedding feast hosted by Zeus and threw a golden apple into the crowd. It was inscribed with the word *kallisti,* meaning "for the fairest." In order to settle the ensuing quarrel among Aphrodite, Hera, and Athena as to who should win this first beauty contest, Zeus decreed that a young man named Paris be the judge. Hera offered him political power and Athena infinite wisdom, but Paris opted for Aphrodite's bribe of marriage to Helen of Troy, reputedly the world's most beautiful woman. However, Helen was already married, and legend has it that her abduction by Paris led eventually to the Trojan War.

The discovery of a new planet is always significant. Alice Howell notes in her book, *The Heavens Declare: Astrological Ages and the Evolution of Consciousness*, that it "looks as if a new planet is discovered when humanity is ready to evolve to the process it represents" (p. 235). She is speaking here of the outer planets, unknown to the ancients, whose discoveries seemed to correlate with new archetypal dynamics in the collective. Pluto, for example, was discovered about the time quantum physics with all its revolutionary ramifications was developing. Archetypally, Pluto is associated with such deep and subconscious transformative processes as sex and rebirth.

Howell also writes about the necessity for human beings to descend into the depths and meet the Shadow, the dark feminine, if we are to withdraw our unconscious projections of that Shadow and evolve in consciousness. It is significant to note that the existence of dark energy/matter was scientifically proven just when Eris was discovered. Might her discovery at the dawn of the twenty-first century suggest that humanity is ready to evolve in relationship to the dark feminine and our collective Shadow? Might it be time to recover the power and beauty of the feminine that has been relegated to the underworld by patriarchal structures? Might we also be ready to explore the enhanced dimensions and possibilities of human consciousness suggested by quantum physics, which has been around for almost a century now and is being utilized by almost all our technologies? Might we awaken to the implications of this so-called "quantum consciousness" and begin to sense our essential oneness with all that is?

As potential herald of a new era, Eris is a most interesting astronomical body. She is an outsider whose orbit is far off the elliptic and far out on the edges of the known solar system. She moves among the wildly strange community of trans-Neptunian objects about which very little is known. As one among many, Eris might be seen archetypally as a potential teacher of relationships and, with the second shiniest surface of any body orbiting our sun, as the great reflector or illuminator of the consequences of our false values and actions. Mythically, she represents the uninvited but unafraid, relentless, truth-revealing feminine, feared and avoided in many stories but a wise and powerful guide in others. Her well-known myth of the golden apple demonstrates that *everyone must be invited to the party—everyone must have a seat at the table* or strife and chaos result. Exclusion never works, and self-centered greed leads ultimately to war.

Other myths about Eris add to the multidimensionality of her archetype and provide provocative clues as to her meaning for our times. According to some accounts, she was the daughter of Zeus and Hera, thus a sister and sometimes companion to warlike Mars. She was said to be the mother of the troublesome daughters released from Pandora's box, including Dysnomia (Lawlessness), the name given to the new planet's moon. This makes her also the mother of Hope, who remained locked in the box but who is sorely needed nowadays. Eris was seen as the goddess of hard work, healthy competition, and doing one's best for something that matters. Finally, Eris was considered so powerful that when Zeus wanted to reverse the course of the sun for a day in order to settle a dispute, she was the goddess he called upon for help.

All archetypes have both a dark and a light side. Eris's darker associations have long been emphasized, but we will have to pay close attention to what is unfolding in this era in order to understand her full potential—in order to reclaim the whole range of the feminine and bring it back into balance with the long-unbridled masculine. The Eris archetype is powerful enough to bring about the demotion of Pluto and complex enough to symbolize the many processes with which we must engage if we are to survive as a species now that the precariousness of life on our planet is obvious. The fact that she takes 560 years to complete a single orbit around the sun signifies the depth of the work needed.

Once Eris was discovered, I read every article about her I could find. Eventually, two scholarly and astrologically detailed books were published: *Discovering Eris: The Symbolism and Significance of a New Planetary Archetype*, by Keiron Le Grice, and *The Tenth Planet: Revelations from the Astrological Eris*, by Henry Seltzer. Among other details about the planet, these authors consider such mythic qualities of Eris as her unabashed confrontation with the powers that be in order to bring about a more balanced and transformative justice. Le Grice focuses on her connections with the evolution of the self and the movement to a deeper level of consciousness and unity because of her archetypal relationship with dark energy. Seltzer points out her relative significance in the astrological charts of various justice seekers and agents of change, as well as in charts of several actors who have portrayed warriors for justice. I devoured these two books and in late 2017, returned to Seltzer's book. My feeling of connection with the Eris archetype and its importance for our times reemerged.

During the night of January 6, 2018, Epiphany, I dreamed that I urgently needed to explain my sense of being called as a woman priest to help heal our troubled world. My lengthy response in the dream was so passionate that it woke me up and left me afire with the conviction that I had to pay attention. Although I couldn't remember my exact responses in the dream, I knew they implied that the purpose of my life and work was still to be in the arena of restoring justice and balance regarding gender, race, class, religion, ethnicity—everything dividing the human family. Since I had just finished rereading *The Tenth Planet*, Eris's justice-warrior archetype was in my mind. I was also thinking that in my astrological chart she is in the third house of communication, which includes writing (see Appendix A). I sensed that I was being called to write something about Eris in the light of my passion for justice and the toxicity of our times, but I resisted that idea. I did not want to take on a task that seemed so challenging and disruptive of my fairly quiet, mostly retired life.

In the couple of hours of inner dialogue and wrestling that followed—before I finally got up and started jotting down notes—many threads wove together, and the idea of this book was born. It would be the personal story of my many awakenings—including my awakening to the archetype of Eris—and also of the awakenings I see going on around us in this new era of the twenty-first century. I knew I would need to write it as a story, both a playfully honest and deadly serious account, but a story, not a treatise. I wanted it to carry the truth of my heart as well as of my head in hopes that such an offering would stimulate insights for others into their own awakenings. Since the seeds of inner growth come from countless sources, this would simply be a casting forth of my own seeds in service of life and greater consciousness in these difficult times.

By way of creative synchronicities, confirmation immediately started coming my way. In the next morning's e-mail of Richard Rohr's reflections for the day, I read about the importance for each of us to bear witness to our own truth, our own story. Next, my e-mailed Enneagram reading for Fives, my type, warned me to stay real and personal instead of giving in to the temptation of my type to be scholarly. I then *happened* to go to church that morning, which I don't always do, and in his sermon the priest urged us to *pay attention* to our epiphanies, our inspirations, and to take up pen and paper and write them down. "Write and keep track," he kept saying in effect, "of whatever deeply touches you that seems to be coming from beyond you. These are revelations, treasures for your soul, and you have to *write them down!*"

All my life, people have urged me to write, but I have always avoided the limelight and any self-promotion that might put me on some kind of pedestal. I turned seventy-five in October 2017 and had become increasingly comfortable with my calling at this stage of life to be primarily a contemplative. The question of a call to other possibilities stayed in my awareness, but I was relaxing into it, trusting I would recognize such a call when and if there was one. Then came my epiphany dream, the idea of writing this book, and these affirming synchronicities. But inner resistance and several questions remained. At my age, dare I write my personal story? Dare I try to tell the truths of my life—all of them? Dare I also come out about my interest in astrology and write this book in relation to a newly discovered planet and little-known archetype, Eris, the uninvited goddess? And dare I, a nonscientist, write about the potential significance for our times of quantum consciousness?

Fear and self-doubt were my first all-too familiar responses to the inspiration to do so. Fortunately, on hearing about my book idea, my passionate writer daughter, Amy, gave me Elizabeth Gilbert's book *Big Magic: Creative Living Beyond Fear*. Gilbert says, in effect, "Go for it! Follow any creative idea that grabs you. It is a treasure and you can trust in its magic." In that light, the fact that I am this age means I have a lifetime of awakenings about which to write, so maybe now is exactly the right time. Serendipitously, I also had just come across *Who Do We Choose to Be? Facing Reality, Claiming Leadership, Restoring Sanity*, the newest book by Margaret J. Wheatley, gifted writer and well-respected researcher of organizational behavior. Given the unsustainable, possibly end stages of current economic, political, and religious structures, Wheatley encourages us to become full-on warriors for the human spirit where we are, as we can, with what we have—a truly Eris-era vision. Right now, this is what *I* have—my story and the powerful lens of this new archetype.

Like everyone, however, I remain a work in progress, unintentionally making mistakes and doing or saying hurtful things. I offer my heartfelt apologies for any places in this book where I have been blind to my white biases, heteronormative assumptions, cultural ignorance, and narrow interpretations of a situation. Please forgive me. I welcome feedback so that I can keep growing.

That being said, this whole book is simply an offering of my personal awakenings and my perspectives on what might be awakening in our times. My hope is that it will stir memories and new insights in readers. I also hope my vision and intuitions about the challenges and demands presented by the emerging archetype of Eris will offer some guidance and encouragement. The mindful gifts and offerings of each of us are sorely needed.

Part I of *The Uninvited Goddess* details the personal story of my many awakenings, beginning with my lifelong hunger for reading and studying and my spiritual awakening as a young girl. I describe some of the many things I learned through college and creating a mixed-race family. Two chapters focus on the experiences that led me to become an Episcopal priest and then led me to open spiritually to all faiths. I go on to tell about helping found Greenfire, a women's retreat center. The concluding chapter discusses my most recent journey as a writer and contemplative.

The first chapter of Part II, Chapter 12, describes some signs of the devastating toxicity of our times, as well as some of its hopeful signs, its awakenings. The concluding chapter, Chapter 13, presents the revelatory possibilities of quantum consciousness. I explore the exciting idea that this archetypal Era of Eris invites—indeed demands—a transformation of consciousness on a broad scale.

For me, Eris's appearance in our solar system summons us to *pay attention* to all that is unjust and wreaking havoc in our times— all that needs to change. This book is primarily an invitation for us to free our minds from entrenched patriarchal patterns for the sake of the earth, to serve life with increasing gratitude wherever we are called, and to participate in the evolution of consciousness in ever-unfolding ways. Eris is the archetype whose time has come, and she is none too soon on the scene.

Welcome, Eris. We desperately need your justice-seeking, feminine-warrior energy now!

Authors Note: In this book I have chosen the option of capitalizing "Black" when used as a designation of race, of peoples of the African diaspora. I do this as a sign of respect for those ripped from their true tribal roots, but also as a sign of protest against the current global resurgence of the white supremacist movement.

Part I

My
Stories
of Awakening

Chapter 1

Beginning with Grief

My first awakening was into grief. I have come to understand that this began in utero less than three months before my birth. At that time, my mother's thirteen-year-old brother, Chester, the only boy and beloved princeling in a family with two older daughters, died a bizarre hanging death in the basement of his home. My grandmother, who had been upstairs fixing his lunch, found him there. The only explanation I have ever heard was that he was practicing rope tricks because he had recently seen a magician doing such tricks. Asking for additional details was always forbidden. Was he perhaps experimenting sexually with autoerotic asphyxiation? I'll never know. In any case, Chester's death was a defining moment for my whole extended family.

My maternal grandmother was the firstborn of three sisters whose parents had emigrated from Sweden to the Boston, Massachusetts, area. My mother was the firstborn of her generation in this close-knit family, and I was the firstborn in mine. Apparently all the grief of Chester's death, as well as all my grandparents' hopes for the future, became focused on me. I have an image of the entire family around my crib, simultaneously caring and crying. Until very recently, when most of my mother's cousins have died, I never attended a family gathering without being told by one of them, "If you hadn't been born, your grandparents never would have survived!" This was a daunting narrative to place on a little girl—and a powerfully formative story for the grown woman.

Now mine is hardly the worst wounded-womb story in this world of war, famine, refugees, and oppression. In fact, perhaps the majority of births are into grief, trauma, violence, poverty, or some kind of craziness. But all of us have to probe the depths of our own story to become free enough to live the fullest life we can. At least *I* needed to do that, but it was deep work and took me a long time. As I grew up and learned more about structures of oppression, my grief seemed to grow. It felt much older and bigger than my little life—as if connected to the Middle Passage, to slavery, racism, and lynching, to witch hunts and burnings, to female circumcision and foot-binding, to all "power-over" systems and structures everywhere throughout time. And it felt way too big to hold.

I was driven to pursue the roots of grief in my own story, to do healing work around that, and to open more fully to the liberation and compassion of the universe, which I also experienced. Insight came one day in the late 1970s as I was reading Agnes Sanford's book, *The Healing Light.* I followed her suggestion of dropping meditatively into my past to discover when I first became unhappy. But I couldn't remember ever being truly happy. So I went back and back, until I came, in utero, to Chester's death, and I knew this was the root cause that needed release. I tell this story now in relation to Eris, the uninvited goddess, and my journey of awakening because it gives a context for my empathic sense of grief and compassion for all suffering and injustice—any time, that is, that I pay attention enough to see and feel it, which, sadly, isn't often enough.

I was born during the global grief and trauma of the Second World War. My dad was in the U.S. Army, stationed on Cape Cod instead of being sent overseas because as a young boy he had lost an eye. My mom and I lived for several months with my grandparents in their little house in Roslindale, Massachusetts, but eventually we moved with Dad into army housing in Falmouth on Cape Cod. We had a small unit in a few rows of units just a block from the ocean. This is the first home I can remember. There I learned to love the sea with its roar and salty smell and to delight in boats and sandy, shell-strewn beaches. There I also learned to love seafood, especially lobster, although I remember being terrified of the wildly waving claws and many creepy legs of the creatures before they were plunged to their death in boiling water. I have many other enduring childhood memories of quintessential New England scenes. In one, I was just walking down a street with my dad on a snowy evening when I suddenly became mesmerized by the large, fluffy flakes dancing in the glow of an old streetlamp. I stopped in my tracks to gaze at this enchanting, somewhat mystical scene.

So here I was, this girl-child growing up in a working- to middle-class white family in the greater Boston area, being doted on by her maternal grandparents and her close aunts and uncles. Initially, I starred in that role because, along with being the only child for several years, I was apparently gifted verbally. The oft-repeated example was that I was able to recite the whole of Clement Clarke Moore's poem *Twas the Night Before Christmas* at the age of three (I was often told the age of two, but that doesn't seem possible). Early on, however, all the attention overwhelmed me, and I withdrew into shyness, into introversion. In fact, a couple of years later, I became a nursery school dropout because I couldn't bear the playful extroversion required in that setting. I can still feel the awkwardness and angst of sitting alone on the sidelines during activities. One time, I "won" a pair of sunglasses, which must have been a kind of booby prize because I hadn't even joined the game. I remember hiding them so I didn't have to tell my mother and grandmother about them when they came to pick me up.

Years passed before I sorted out why I dreaded public attention, especially any kind that seemed to put me on a pedestal. In fact, I still almost never go to movies or restaurants on my own. I did know from a young age that any kind of limelight felt dangerous and that this probably had to do with my mother. My earliest memories of our relationship feel tense, fraught with underlying conflict. This became particularly apparent once my brother David, two and a half years younger, was born. I adored him but, all too soon, became jealous of Mom's preferential treatment of him. This eventually became explicit in such pleas to me as, "Why can't you be more like David? He's so loving and warm while you are so closed and cold."

Now, David was a very cuddly kid, whereas I tended to stand back and observe more. Also, he was younger and cried more readily if we were fighting, as siblings do. In any case, I distinctly remember thinking to myself, *How can Mom say that about me? It's not fair and it's not true! I'm not cold. I do care about things, lots of things.*

I have a ton of feelings all the time. Like right now, she is making me really mad! And she's making me very sad. I want to yell. And I want to cry. Why can't she see this? How can she call me cold?

In many of the countless photographs of me from babyhood through nursery school, however, I can see the cautious, somewhat distant child Mom must have seen. In one such photo, I am standing on my grandparents' couch amid the mountain of stuffed animals I had been given by my adoring relatives, but there is a somewhat suspicious frown on my face and a withdrawn stance to my body. That frown shows up in pictures over and over again for years. There were physical manifestations of that facial expression, too. For example, I would get stomachaches every Sunday during our ritual dinner at my grandparents' house. I see this now as a bodily reaction to the tension between their doting and Mom's criticisms.

In time, Mom also began labeling me "lazy" whenever she thought I was procrastinating on chores. For example, every Saturday I was to do a housecleaning task like vacuuming, plus an outdoor task like weeding. But I wanted to relax for a while into the Saturday break from the routine of school first. Usually that meant I wanted to sit in my favorite chair in the living room and read. If Mom saw me there, she'd say, "You are supposed to be doing your chores now, not reading!"

"Mom," I'd respond, "I promise I'll get to that job in a bit."

But she would say, "You're just being lazy. You need to do your chores when I tell you to do them, not in your own sweet time!"

I remember thinking that Mom got on me about chores *whenever* she saw me sitting and reading, so I felt rebellious. I also remember thinking that the tasks I was assigned were often much harder or more boring than those assigned to David. I was clearly in competition with him, and I tried to get him in trouble with Mom whenever I could. For example, if she came upon us fighting, I would say, "David started it!" If something got broken, I would swear, "That was David's fault, not mine. He knocked it over." I became a really good liar, which didn't feel good.

It is not surprising, in retrospect, that I gradually shut down, withdrew, and probably withheld affection around Mom. I don't know the extent to which her *cold* label of me preceded or followed my emotional withdrawal from her, but in many ways the *lazy* label was justified in that I spent as much of my time as possible escaping, reading books and fantasizing. Eventually, the punishment Mom found most effective was to say that I couldn't read for some period of time.

Over the years, I was able to get a fuller picture of all these dynamics. I came to understand that Mom had been belittled and somewhat tyrannized by her father, the grandfather who doted on me—a clear set-up for jealousy. Furthermore, although she was extremely smart and capable, her options in life were limited simply because she was a woman of her times with a working-class background. So Mom brought to motherhood a complex set of issues and insecurities that helped set the stage for her reactions to me. But I know now that she was also trying to help me by molding me into a sweeter, more compliant little girl—into one who might have an easier time in life than she had had. By contrast, Mom's relationship with my brothers, David and Rick, seven years younger than me, was quite loving and straightforward. David tells me that he always knew he was beloved. Mom was a safe mother to him, whereas she didn't feel safe to me until many years had passed and much healing had happened.

The saga of this introverted, somewhat sad and fearful girl-child has its other side, too. Throughout those early years, my awakening imagination was flourishing in a rich inner world of fear and fantasy, mystery and delight, of gods, goddesses, and fairy tales. I remember reading everything I could get my hands on, even comic books, my favorite of which—no surprise—was Wonder Woman. I especially loved book collections like The Bobbsey Twins and the Nancy Drew mystery series, many of which were tucked away on a shelf in the little back bedroom of my grandparents' home. My forever-favorite book, though, was *The Blue Fairy Book*, a collection of fairy tales edited by Andrew Lang and first published in 1889. My copy is quite dog-eared and falling apart at the binding. It may even be a very early edition because the title page has no date. Its thirty-nine mostly familiar stories are told in exquisite detail in the tiniest font over 390 pages, a lot to devour and savor! I especially loved "Beauty and the Beast," the familiar story of a young girl shut up with a gentle beast in a lovely fantasy castle full of all kinds of delights, especially books. It is a tale of withdrawal, loneliness, compassion, love, and transformation—a tale I later came to view as a reflection of many of my own inner dynamics.

I wonder now if reading offered not only an escape from loneliness and grief but also an early container in which the complexities of life could be considered and held. I don't remember reading about Eris, but surely I came across the myth of the origins of the Trojan War, and surely I was quite aware of the tragedies war brought having been born during World War II. The archetypal realm, as I would now call it, was already calling to me.

Along with reading and trying to learn more about anything that caught my attention, I grew increasingly entranced by beautiful words and meaningful sentences. I soon began copying excerpts on little cards, collecting maybe hundreds of such treasures over the years and returning to them often. I also spent much of my alone time daydreaming. I remember imagining that I was an angel and could fly as I floated up and down the stairs with a flowing scarf for wings. I made up stories, too, which soon became romantic visions of true love complete with cuddles and kisses.

Another early, somewhat magical experience had to do with discovering what is called "lucid dreaming." In childhood, I had recurring nightmares of being attacked by wild animals like lions, tigers, and occasionally bears. I remember trying for a long time to reassure myself that these were just dream animals, so they couldn't hurt me. Then one night, I recognized that I was dreaming and instead of running away decided I should speak to the animals. In my dream, I went up to them and even patted them. They in turn welcomed and rubbed up against me. When I awoke, I was ecstatic about the experience because I felt so empowered and so grateful that I would never need to fear my dreams again. It was a private revelation, an awakening into some deeply centered part of myself that I hadn't known was there. I can't say I have had many such dramatic experiences of lucid dreaming over the years, although I think it was involved in several flying dreams because I can remember convincing myself in these dreams that I really could fly. In later years, it was an aspect of some spiritually meaningful dreams in which I chose to stay with the experiences or to follow the images more closely.

Other special early memories include going to Revere Beach, or sometimes Crane's Beach, for the day with the extended family and being totally entranced by the ocean. I remember hours of playing and daydreaming there on the sandy shore and then eating sandwiches of freshly picked tomatoes and scrumptious cheese, slightly melted by the heat and smushed from the picnic basket. On longer outings to Cape Cod, I remember loving those beaches, too, and our meals of fried clams, French fries, and boiled lobster from one of the lobster shacks around, as common then as hot dog stands today. For family vacations, we always rented lakeside cottages, usually in New Hampshire. In these settings, I learned to swim, row a boat by myself, and delight in the quiet beauty of woods and water.

At one childhood home in Methuen, Massachusetts, our property abutted some woods, and I played there for hours, alone or with a few friends, in all kinds of make-believe games. In this spirit of adventure, once we had a television, my favorite show was *Flash Gordon, Space Explorer*, and, much later, *Xena, Warrior Princess*. I became a bit of a tomboy and loved exerting myself physically in both neighborhood games and the few sports then open to girls. Also, despite the fact that I was competing with David for Mom's favor, we played together a lot and by adulthood became true soul mates. I had prayed for a sister before my second brother, Rick, was born, but I adored him at first sight and loved caring for him. Nowadays, we three siblings, retired and scattered around the country, talk together with our spouses on Skype for an hour or so every month and get together whenever we can.

I suspect that all my early reading and inner reflection gave me an edge in grade school—indeed, probably all along in school. For example, my second-grade teacher had a combined classroom that included third grade. I don't remember anything special about that year except that I liked the teacher, but apparently I completed the work of both groups. Consequently, when the year ended, I was promoted to the fourth grade, presumably so I wouldn't be bored. Since my October birthday already made me one of the youngest students in my grade, overnight I became almost two years younger than most of my classmates. I was always fairly tall, so didn't look younger, but my parents would later use my age to set strict limits on my social life. It was my senior year before I was old enough to take driving lessons, so I was dependent on others for rides forever, it seemed. Then I graduated from high school and started college at sixteen, which is a little appalling to me now as I consider my sixteen-year-old grand-daughters! I've jumped way ahead in my story here, but it is significant to note how apparently small circumstances in the life of a child, like being in a combined class, can have big ramifications.

So I had a rich childhood despite my underlying sense of grief and ongoing mother conflict. It formed a complex but solid foundation for my life and for my later attraction to the Eris archetype. My lifelong sense of curiosity, my delight in beauty, my hunger for meaning, and my compassion for the outsider were all in full flower.

Chapter 2

Seeking the Missing Key

When I was about to enter fifth grade, my dad got transferred to Minneapolis, Minnesota. We said goodbye to our Boston relatives and to our familiar New England environment, an uprooting that was difficult for us all, but particularly traumatic for my mom. She survived by making weekly phone calls to her mother and sister, and every summer, either we went back to Boston or Mom's parents and her sister's family visited us.

In the summer before seventh grade, while we were in Boston staying with my grandparents, I suddenly got very sick. I was soon diagnosed with nephritis and placed in Boston Children's Hospital. Nephritis is a serious disease in which the kidney walls break down. Part of the treatment, in those days, at least, was the severe limitation of any physical activity at all in order to protect the kidneys while they healed. Even going up or down stairs more than once or twice a day was forbidden.

That whole stretch of time is a bit of a blur in my memory, although I do remember how much I dreaded my all-too-frequent doctor's visits because the nurse always needed to draw blood. And I remember how my grandmother doted on me. For example, I wasn't supposed to consume any sodium, but she happily gave me the sandwiches I craved—made from canned, undoubtedly salty, Boston baked beans.

After several weeks, I was allowed to fly home to Minneapolis, but I had to be homeschooled until the end of April that school year. My tutor was an elderly gentleman and an excellent teacher who encouraged all my interests. In many ways, I quite loved those months because they were so private, so devoted to books and learning—not unlike Beauty's time in the magical castle of the Beast. Also, I was very ill and weak, so physical activity wasn't at all inviting. In any case, I don't remember being bored or even lonely. At first, a few of my grade-school friends would visit, but as time went on and they became more involved in a school life that I couldn't share, their visits dropped away. Solitude became my normal state. When I was finally able to return to school, I remember how lost and scared I felt upon entering our really big junior high. By that time most of the cliques were well established, so to use phrases I ascribe to the Eris archetype, I was an outsider and longed to be invited to some parties or included at some lunchroom table. I wanted to be one of the gang.

Fortunately, we lived in a neighborhood with many kids and lots of street games and evening hang-out sessions. Mom and Dad developed friendships with several neighboring families, too. One delightful family down the block had similarly been transferred away from their roots, so we always spent holidays together at one home or the other. They were a Roman Catholic family and had two sons close to my age. Across the street was another Catholic family with one son my age. These guys all went to a Catholic boys' school so were quite interested in the few girls in our neighborhood, which added a fair bit of spice to my life. Come ninth grade, they and their friends were my first dates, and one of their friends took me to my first semiformal dance and gave me my first kiss—in the movie *Kismet!*

To make up for the fact that I had gotten sick on that visit to Boston, my folks let me go back on my own the summer after eighth grade. I lived with my grandparents for the month of July, though I also spent a lot of time with my aunt's family and three younger cousins. For the month of August, we all stayed at a rental cottage in West Yarmouth on the Cape. That was a magical summer for me because I was budding into adolescence, being doted on by everyone, and loving the wonder of ocean beaches and "summertime in old Cape Cod." Part of the daily schedule for this Swedish family who delighted in sweets was a morning coffee break accompanied by assorted fresh donuts or sweet rolls. Then, every afternoon we went to the nearby Dairy Queen for a treat. My very favorite became a mocha frappe, as milkshakes were called in Boston. We also surely had desserts at every meal and possibly late-night snacks, although I don't remember that. I blissfully enjoyed it all, with nary a thought to the consequences of such habits.

I'll never forget my mother's expression as I entered the reception area after my flight home. Her smile of welcome quickly morphed into a disapproving frown, almost as though she didn't quite recognize me. Then she said something like, "What happened to you? You must have gained ten pounds!"

I didn't know how to respond, and I probably pulled back from hugging her—in a manner deserving of that old "cold" label. I knew my clothes were all a little tight, but I hadn't really thought about weight. I was just aware of growing up, of my body changing and my breasts blossoming. Such changes were welcome, weren't they? But was I also becoming fat?

Mom continued to make comments about eating and weight. "Judy, you shouldn't be eating any more of that dessert."

"That's not fair," I'd say. "Everyone else is eating more."

"But it's fattening, and you don't want to gain more weight!"

I soon started feeling quite self-conscious about my body, although I was probably a pretty average size. The truth is that none of our eating habits at home were that great. Those were the days of store-bought fluffy white bread served with oleomargarine that came in plastic bags into which you had to squeeze orangish food coloring, dinners of mostly meat and potatoes, and always a dessert. Nobody knew much about nutrition. My dad loved late-night snacks, too, and I often joined him. Ice cream became my forever downfall. All of this laid the foundation for lifelong problems with diet and weight. However, it took until college and the increasing cult of thinness for the disorder to develop fully—and many more years for me to understand and deal with its roots.

During this time of budding puberty with its accompanying issues and insecurities, I was fortunate to find a dear soul-mate friend, Toni, who shared some of my introverted patterns and predilections. We met in the eighth grade and stayed close through ninth grade. Together, Toni and I studied and pondered the sadness and emptiness of our mostly middle-class and white world, although we had not yet awakened to the realities of either. We were also, of course,

World War II babies, so we knew in our bones and from stories about wartime suffering. The ills of Pandora's box seemed all too prevalent.

Toni and I would often meet up halfway between our homes at the base of the Washburn Park Water Tower, although at the time we didn't know its name. To us it was just the "water tower"—a massive domed concrete structure perched atop a hill in the center of a tangled warren of streets with big houses and giant old trees. This 110-foot-high tower is still a significant but quite secluded landmark in South Minneapolis. It boasts eight sculpted eagles spaced around the top, each with an eight-foot wingspan. Beneath each eagle is an eighteen-foot-tall bas relief, "Guardian of Health"—a robed and helmeted, downward-gazing figure with his hands resting on the hilt of a huge sword, which points to the ground. Toni and I would climb up the hill and sit beneath the feet of one of these figures, under the tip of its majestic sword, to dream our adolescent dreams and ask our deepest questions of one another and the world.

Thoughts flowed wildly and freely between us. We were of one mind with our shared concerns, which included the following.

"You know, I don't think my parents are particularly happy. What about yours?"

"Mine don't seem happy either...in fact, I can't think of any adults who seem very happy. They just worry about work, bills, their kids...everything."

"They must all have had some happiness as children, though, don't you think?"

"I would think so...but the two of us are pretty sad a lot of the time."

"True...but we also love to be together talking, and we love reading, nature, and all sorts of beautiful things."

"Yes, and we look forward to some things in the future, like going off to college. That will be really exciting!"

"Right! And traveling to exotic places..."

"Falling in love must be the best...and getting married someday..."

"But then think what happens. I see all the mothers in my neighborhood out in their backyards hanging diapers on their clotheslines day after day. They talk to one another, but there doesn't seem to be much joy in it all."

"I agree! So, what do you think it's all about, then—life, growing up?"

"I think there must be something more, some missing key, some meaning we don't know about, don't you?"

"Yes! I think otherwise more people would decide just to eat, drink, be merry, and die young!"

"Maybe it's something so private that people just never talk about it. At least, I've never heard any adults talk about what gives their lives meaning."

"Me neither. Or…maybe they figured it out once but then forgot about it."

"Maybe so…but do you really think they did figure it out?"

"Some of them must have. How could they stand to go on otherwise?"

"Well, do you think *we'll* figure it out?? That we'll find that missing key of some meaning to life?"

"I think we have to help each other keep on looking until we do!"

"Yes! But…what if we start to forget as we get older?"

"Well, let's write letters to our older selves so we don't ever forget!"

"Great idea!! We can bring paper and pencils whenever we get together. We'll write all our questions down and keep the letters so our more grownup selves will remember what really matters."

"And maybe someday we'll discover that missing key, and then we'll really have something to write about!!"

And that is what we did—wrote letters about all our questions and concerns and about our quest for what we named The Missing Key to the Meaning of Life. Sometimes we did this at the water tower and sometimes in one another's homes. I remember that we spent many hours, and probably many sleepovers, in the basement rec room of our house, huddled side by side on the floor, backs to the wall, with our paper and pencils. In winter weather or on rainy days, we surely found shelter indoors, but my strongest memory of the setting for our get-togethers is that midpoint meeting place of the tower, where we sat, similarly huddled together, under the sword of a towering but gentle guardian figure, with a giant eagle hovering over us the whole time.

One of the sad facts of my life is that at some point, perhaps around the time I went off to college, the possibility of anyone reading these letters was so embarrassing to me that I destroyed them all. Much, much later, while doing doctoral work in feminist liberation theology and ministry, I encountered the writing of Carol Gilligan, the Harvard professor who documented that, by around twelve to thirteen years of age, young girls start shedding their powerful younger selves in service of cultural norms and gender stereotypes, i.e., in service of boys. Her signature book on the subject is *In a Different Voice: Psychological Theory and Women's Development.* I met Carol once at a conference, and she got quite excited when I told her that my friend and I had actually documented an awareness of that pending loss of self when we were about twelve. Then I had to confess to her that I had destroyed all my letters. A second sad fact of my life is that Toni died of breast cancer a few years ago, just before I was expecting to reconnect with her at our fiftieth high school reunion. She lived in the Boston area by then, and I lived relatively nearby in Maine, but I had waited too long to reach out to her.

My questioning work with Toni did, however, lead me to perhaps my most life-changing awakening—a spiritual awakening. As an eclectic and avid reader, I consumed several of the many novels available about the early Christian era. I never connected any of these stories with my search for the missing key, however, until I read *The Robe,* by Lloyd C. Douglas. Along with offering a tantalizing picture of Jesus's words and ministry, this is a romantic story of true love—all powerful stuff for a young adolescent girl who had grown up in a liberal, somewhat heady but quite uninspiring Congregational Church setting. In the novel, the young centurion who cast lots for and won Jesus's robe after the crucifixion is so haunted by the whole event that he goes on a search for everything he can learn about Jesus. He eventually becomes a follower, a Christian. His true love is a favorite in the Roman court, but she soon joins him in this new faith. The climactic scene is of the two of them heading off *into the clouds*—as pictured in the movie based on the novel—to be put to death by the emperor because they would not renounce their faith. In the story, for them this is a glorious, not a tragic, finale because they have chosen to be faithful to the end, together.

What grabbed me in the gut, heart, soul, head, everywhere as I read this ending was that somehow the faith that the centurion and his love had found was worth dying for, despite their unconsummated romance. It seemed as clear as day to me as I finished the book—in tears, of course—that something worth dying for was certainly something worth living for, and I wanted it! My whole being was saying *Yes!* to this Jesus, this God, this sense of *Presence* that seemed to encompass and fill my room and me. Surely here was the missing key Toni and I had been seeking. For a couple of hours, I felt caught up and held—embraced—by meaning. I cried, rejoiced, prayed—all the things one does when having a soul-deep awakening. I couldn't believe we had been on our quest for so long but it had never occurred to either one of us that our missing key might have something to do with God. After all, we had both grown up in churchgoing families. I resolved then and there to get to know this faith, this Jesus, and to give myself to this spiritual path that seemed so full of love and meaning even in the face of death.

Then I had to figure out how to tell Toni what I had discovered. I was at a loss as to how to do that because I didn't really know anything yet and because I had never heard anyone describe this kind of experience. Furthermore, it had all been quite mystical, quite beyond words. I finally decided that we should go canoeing, one of our favorite things to do together, so that I could have a stretch of private time to tell her the story of *The Robe*. Then I planned to read her the last chapter of the book in hopes that it would speak to her as it had to me.

So early one lovely late-spring Saturday, my mom drove Toni and me to nearby Lake Calhoun, where we booked a canoe for a long outing. We paddled leisurely into a secluded area, and then just started drifting along in the warm sunshine. I recounted for Toni the story of the centurion who won Jesus's robe, his quest to learn more about Jesus, his eventual commitment as a believer, his true love in Rome, and the emperor's obsession with persecuting Christians. Then I read her the last chapter of the book, glancing up at her periodically, hoping to see signs that she was "getting it." When I finished, Toni sighed, and with tears in her eyes, said, "Oh, yes! I see what you mean about our missing key!"

"I'm so glad!" I said. "I didn't know how I could tell you about it without reading this to you."

"That was perfect, Jude. Thank you!"

"I'm so relieved. Oh, Toni, we have so much more to discover together, but now we know where to look. Can you believe, though, that we never thought our missing key might have something to do with God?"

"I can't believe it," she said. "I'm still kind of numb, but thoughts of God never occurred to me, and here I am, a Catholic who goes to church every Sunday!"

"I go to church regularly, too," I answered. "I guess neither of us saw any connections between what we do on Sunday mornings and the rest of our lives."

We then spent some time talking about the book with its moving romantic story and dramatic ending. We talked about a faith that could outshine even the tragedy of death and loss. And we shared our excitement about the unexpected place to which our quest for the missing key had brought us.

At some point, Toni asked, "Well, what do you think we should do now?"

I answered, "I've thought about maybe reading my Bible or talking to our minister...but I don't really know."

"Me neither," she said.

We finished our canoe ride with some conversation and lots of reflective silence. I felt deeply satisfied by Toni's response to my fumbling attempt to share my revelation with her, but the truth is that we didn't have much of a chance to follow up on our respective journeys after that. Life intervened, as they say. Maybe the fact that we were looking at Christianity from quite different perspectives had something to do with it. Also, Toni's dearly beloved and most respected father died unexpectedly around that time, and that changed everything for her. Furthermore, this was the summer before we entered high school, when the onset of dating, along with changing circles of friends, meant we rarely got together anymore. So my story since that most significant friendship and life-changing experience will unfold here, but sadly I know very little of Toni's story.

My spiritual awakening the day I finished *The Robe* was indeed an experience beyond and deeper than words, but I want to try to wrap some words around it. After all, this is a book about paying attention to life and awakenings, and this was a primal experience for me, a conversion moment. It set the tone for all the awakenings to come in that it was a personal encounter with the Other, the great mystery I had been seeking, although I hadn't known what I was seeking. All I knew was that Toni and I were asking the truly big questions: Why live? What is the meaning of life given the reality of human suffering? Yes, we were young, and yes, our world was small. We knew next to nothing about true suffering on the grand or global scale. But our search was genuine and from the depths of our young souls. I experienced an encounter with the Other, the Holy, that was just as deep and genuine, embracing the great paradox of both the pain and the joy of life.

I've discovered since that perhaps everyone has these moments of awe, beauty, joy, awareness, love, *Knowing*—these undeniable, utterly surprising moments when one is taken out of oneself into something bigger, into Mystery. Yet we are all mostly silent about these times, and so maybe most of them fade into the landscape of our lives and don't seem to change anything. In later life, I was privileged to hear about these kinds of moments from many people, but as a young girl that day, all I knew was that for me this was *Real*. I probably wouldn't have proclaimed "There is a God," because those words weren't part of my life. But I might have said "There is Meaning," because I experienced it and knew it through my whole being. I had an *I—Thou* encounter, as described by theologian Martin Buber in his book *I and Thou*, and the truth of it has never left me.

I'm thinking now that the impact of it all for me was probably in direct proportion to the persistence of the searching Toni and I had done. We dared to follow our curiosity wherever it led and to ask the universe, so to speak, the deepest of questions. I then experienced the universe meeting me at the deepest of levels, the level of Presence. That encounter said to me that the universe is full of meaning and worth a lifelong journey of exploration.

So I say, speak your truth to the universe, to your *god-gods-God* or to your sense of *there's-nothing-out-there*. Follow your curiosity and ask your questions, *all* your questions. Voice your anger, your sadness, your longings, and your uncertainties. Don't be afraid. We human beings are all about communication and connection. Perhaps what we are actually here for is to commune with the cosmos, to probe the heavens and the depths. We are conscious, curious, questioning animals, not the *only* conscious ones on this planet, but certainly the ones most in need of help.

Don't just ask your questions, though. Pay close attention to what comes your way. Listen to your big dreams—or all your dreams, if you are so inclined. Notice real-life scenes and people that grab you, touch you at some level. If you are a reader, heed literature that captures your attention, and, if you are not a reader, consider beginning that practice. Daydreaming and meditation can also take you to powerful places. Eventually perhaps, as Rilke suggests, if we truly live our questions, we will discover one day that we have lived into the answers.

Chapter 3

Surviving High School

The search for the meaning of life led to a huge awakening for me, but there were many more awakenings ahead. One big category has been my ever-evolving journey with Christianity. Not long after my experience with *The Robe* launched me into the commitment to learn about Jesus, God, and the Bible, I became involved in Young Life, an evangelical Christian outreach to high school young people, which was just beginning in Minneapolis at Washburn, my high school, during my sophomore year.

My mother initially urged me to get involved in Young Life because she had heard about it from some church friends and thought it would be good for me. Our relationship had become increasingly strained as I entered adolescence. A typical conversation between us went something like this:

"You're always criticizing me, Mom. It seems like everything I do makes you mad. Plus you say no to everything I ask for."

"Well, Judy, you never even talk to me unless you want something. And you avoid me or give me nasty looks most of the time. What do you expect?"

"I am *not* always asking for something, Mom! I do have friends I want to see, and sometimes I really need something, but that's not all the time!"

"It feels like it to me, and you are certainly avoiding me all the time or giving me that nasty look."

"What nasty look?"

"That look right there, like I'm not even a person and don't have any feelings."

"Well, it seems like my feelings don't matter to you and like everything I do or say just makes you mad!"

"That's not fair, Judy! And you shouldn't talk back to me like that!"

Such encounters might escalate until I either was sent to my room or stormed off there on my own accord. The truth is that I *knew* I was snubbing Mom in that awful way young teenage girls can do. I also knew that I was hurt and totally frustrated by our relationship. We were stuck in a cyclical pattern that had a long history. Furthermore, I was my parents' first teenager, so I had the role of forging the path for my brothers.

As for my dad, he was out of his depth with us, being an utterly honest, simple, grounded, peaceful guy who had long since shut down his own emotional storms. His mother had died when he was a baby. He had been told that it was because he got a cold that she then caught while taking care of him, and it killed her—a terrible message for a little child to carry. His father, who eventually became a speculative dealer in the grain exchange and possibly an alcoholic, also lost a second wife and eventually had a third marriage. I never got the sense that he was much of a father to his three children—my father, his older sister, and a much younger half-brother. So Dad left home to be on his own by about age sixteen. He did go to business school and was fairly successful work-wise, but all his emotional life became focused on my mom, whom he adored. He also loved my two brothers and me unequivocally, although I later doubted he had many emotional reserves left over to give to our children, his grandchildren.

Dad was never able to prevent the battles that arose between the two emotionally charged, deep-thinking females with whom he lived, but he often tried to resolve them. Many, many times when I had taken to my room following an intense argument with Mom, Dad would come in, sit down on the chair by my bed, and say something like, "Honey, your mom doesn't like it any better than you when these fights happen."

I might respond, "Well then, why does she always say no before I even have a chance to explain what I'm asking?"

"Well," he'd say, "she's just worried because you are so much younger than the other kids." Or "She doesn't know those people."

Or "It will be past your curfew." Or something else along these lines. Whenever he could and whatever the issue, though, Dad tried to be a peacemaker. He'd go back and forth between Mom and me seeking resolution, which sometimes happened. In any case, he tried hard, and I think his steadfast caring was a significant and stabilizing rock to me through those difficult years.

At one point, to get help with me, they said, both my parents went to a psychologist. He then asked to meet with me alone. I distinctly remember him explaining to me that my mother was very high-strung, which made sense to me. All her adult life, she'd had trouble with *nerves*, as was often said then of fiery Sagittarian women like her. I remember her going to many doctors for medications, taking to her bed for a day or two periodically, and occasionally even saying that if we didn't behave, she was going to leave us or kill herself. The psychologist told me that it would be good if I could be gentler with Mom. I interpreted this to imply that she was the one with the problem, not I, so *I* needed to be the one mothering *her*. It was a validating experience and probably led to some better behavior on my part, but I was already feeling increasingly guilty about my attitude and actions and was wanting to change.

I should note in this context that during my sophomore year, my unquestioning trust in my dad was broken. From sixth grade until early high school, I had a close friendship with a girl named Susan, who lived two doors down from us. She was a year behind me in school, so probably my age, and as creative and precocious as they come. Her parents were artistic and progressive, so Susan's spacious bedroom was a young girl's delight. She had *stuff* to make almost anything or play any kind of game. We each developed stamp collections, taught ourselves how to play chess, made puppets and wrote plays for them, even started a hand-copied neighborhood newspaper—you name it. If we thought of something, we could pursue it, including going horseback riding, which we both loved.

Sometime in early high school, Susan started spending a lot of time at the stable where we had gone riding. She loved helping out there and apparently developed a relationship with one of the stable hands. Rumors about the nature of that relationship flew. Her parents were worried, and apparently, so were mine. One day when I was standing in the kitchen with Mom and Dad, he said—out of the blue it seemed—"Judy, I've been talking with Mom, and I have decided that I want you to stay away from Susan."

I was startled and horrified. "What do you mean, 'stay away' from her?"

"I don't want you to go over to her house anymore or have her here. She's a bad influence."

"But Dad, she's my friend! That doesn't mean I'm going to do whatever she's doing. We're very different people. She just really needs a friend right now."

"Well, we're worried about you, not her. You are our responsibility, and we don't want you to see her anymore, period!"

"I can't believe you don't trust me and that you think I'd let her be a bad influence on me. Besides, it's not right to avoid someone if they're in some kind of trouble. It's just not right! You have to trust me more than that."

"This is not about trust. It's a decision about your best interests, which is ours to make as your parents. And it's a final decision. You are not to see her anymore!"

That was it. My dad, the rock, wouldn't budge. Nothing I said seemed to touch him or stir his compassion for this girl whose need for support was so obvious to me. Finally, I lost it and went to my room, knowing that something foundational in my life, apart from my newly forming spirituality, had crumbled and that I couldn't trust Dad's counsel anymore. From now on, I would have to rely on my own inner guidance.

With all this going on at home, it's clear why my mother latched onto a Christian outreach program as a lifeline for me, for our relationship, and, indeed, for our whole family. Fortunately, Young Life proved to be quite wonderful. It gave me an exciting and adventurous extracurricular life as well as a context in which to explore Christianity. In those days, Young Life was a young and vital mission, full of humor and deeply compassionate. The leaders were committed to an incarnational, life-on-a-life approach to young people, as well as to founder Jim Rayburn's belief that "It's a sin to bore a kid with the gospel." Weekly school-night club meetings in students' homes would draw fifty or more young people and involve singing, humorous skits, and a message about Jesus. There were occasional weekend camps or outings and a fabulous week-long summer camp.

The summer after my sophomore year, I attended Young Life's Frontier Ranch in Buena Vista, Colorado, with about eight other girls from my class. I was still totally reserved about my nascent spiritual journey, though, and very reticent to discuss it with anyone. I remember how the counselor in our cabin kept trying to meet with me to find out how I was responding to the message, and how I successfully evaded her for most of the week. Eventually, she did get me alone, and I found myself reluctantly telling her about my experience reading *The Robe*. It was the first time I had talked with anyone other than Toni about it and the first time I tried to put the life-changing aspects of that encounter with Presence into words.

Following our conversation, I began connecting the Christian message being preached at the camp with my earlier awakening. Around a campfire on the last night of camp, when the speaker offered us an invitation to stand and share if we'd made a life commitment to follow Jesus, I stood up and did so, truly going public with what up to then had been such a personal and private story. As a result, back home I became involved with the Bible study group offered by our "staff girl," as these adult women were called for way too many years. (The *staff men* were the ones who led up front and gave the talks, while the *staff girls* set up the homes for club meetings, made the notices, and worked with the girls. Such were the times.) These Bible studies were very significant in my life because they gave me a small and caring group of other girls to be part of, and they began to satisfy my desire to learn more about Christianity.

Other than that week at camp, the better part of my summers during high school was spent at the small lake cottage my folks then owned about an hour away from our home in South Minneapolis. We had always rented lakeside cottages for family vacations, but owning this cottage meant we could spend much more time there because Dad could commute. I had mixed feelings about this arrangement. I loved the quiet beauty of the place, but, like all teenagers, I hated being separated from my friends and shut up with my parents and brothers. Fortunately, the family in the neighboring cottage had kids around our ages. They liked to swim, boat, and play card and board games, so we did all those things for hours on end. And I read books, sometimes even out in a boat while my dad or brothers were fishing. It was a great way to avoid the household chores Mom would usually assign if I was lying around inside reading.

I particularly remember one special evening at the lake: I ran away from bickering with Mom or someone else in the cottage and went down to the shore to lie in the bottom of the rowboat tied to our dock. All I could feel was its gentle rocking, all I could hear was the water lapping at its sides, and all I could see was the night sky overhead. It was a magical, mystical time as I watched the shapes of the shifting clouds and the gradual emergence of the stars. It seemed as if the whole show was embracing and calming me, taking me out of my small self into something so much larger and more wonderful. This memory stays with me to this day—a reminder that the world is always inviting us to slow down and pay attention to the mystery present in every moment.

While this was all going on in my family and spiritual journey, I was living high school life in the 1950s. I loved school because I loved learning, and Washburn—a college preparatory public school—had many fantastic teachers. My favorite subjects were chemistry, biology, math, and especially the whole range of English literature. My fascination with the ancient Greco-Roman myths was reawakened, but it would be years before Eris came front and center for me. I had to look to other literary heroines and women warrior figures in those days.

Although my curious and precocious proclivities served me well in academia, they inhibited high school social life. The *pedestals are dangerous places* perception I had felt since early childhood resurfaced. Labels like *too smart* or *the smartest in the class* felt as if they set me apart from my classmates, and I didn't want to feel like the uninvited outsider, the way I felt when I returned to school after being out sick for most of seventh grade. I still wanted desperately just to be one of the gang. I see now how these experiences of feeling marginalized helped pave the way for my attraction to the archetype of Eris and the vision that everyone needs to be invited to the party, everyone needs to be included at the table.

Meantime, I was discovering—awakening to—boys and to all the angst, temptations, and highs that go along with young love. (Note: awakenings can definitely be dangerous passages.) By ninth grade, my crushes were intense and my daydreams extensive, romantic, and sensual. Kissing and physical closeness were, as anticipated, a seductive delight. In retrospect, I was lonely and hungry for love and therefore on a very slippery slope, especially as I got a bit older and more experienced with making out. The mores of my middle-class white world absolutely forbade any petting, not to mention intercourse, and my Christian teaching agreed.

By my junior year, however, I was going too far with my then boyfriend, having given in, bit by bit, to his advances. I was simultaneously scared to death I might get pregnant and increasingly ensnared in the addictive side of sexual activity. My plan, clear as day to me, was that if I got pregnant, I would kill myself. After all, death had never really frightened me. Physically, I developed horrific migraine headaches. I remember playing tennis one day and being almost unable to bend over to pick up a ball. I felt as if my head were being split open by the two realities I was living: smart and spiritually hungry Christian student on the one hand and secret sexual experimenter on the other. Thankfully, I did not get pregnant. I *survived*! And after a year or so, I succeeded in extricating myself from that relationship. However, I didn't share any of this with my Young Life leader, in part because we had a different woman every year (it seemed that they no sooner came on staff in Minneapolis than they got engaged and left to get married), and in part because I was so private about everything. Lord knows I could have benefited from some help!

The blessed thing about this part of my story is that everything was used. The angst, turmoil, and struggles I went through are ubiquitous in some form or another in the life of every adolescent girl, as documented by Carol Gilligan. And the inner work I did to move on from them was an incredible benefit to the work I ended up doing many years later as chaplain and counselor at a boarding school for girls. I have come to trust that this is the nature of the universe. It moves in such a way as to use us and our struggles—somehow, sometime, somewhere—if we do our work and are in a safe enough setting that leans at all toward justice. We may not know it, of course, although we often discover it several years after the fact, but if we are willing to offer ourselves and our truth, very little is for naught. I am trusting that belief even now with the highly personal offering of this book.

Chapter 4

Struggling Through College

In 1959, at age sixteen, I entered Lawrence College (now University) in Appleton, Wisconsin. It was a terrific school, and I thrived on dorm life, a few close friendships, some romances, and many great teachers. I also began the habit of procrastinating on schoolwork, especially studying for exams and writing papers, pulling many all-nighters, a common college activity. Some of my procrastination involved compulsive bridge playing for hours on end in the dorm. So much growing up needs to happen when one is first away from home! I still got excellent grades, so these bad habits were hard to break—until many years later when I went to graduate school with four children at home and could neither bear the inner pressure procrastination brings nor stay up all night.

While I was at Lawrence, about eighty percent of its student body was in a sorority or fraternity. Without knowing much about what it all meant, I rushed and happily was accepted into Kappa Alpha Theta, my sorority of choice. This led to another great awakening—right at the beginning of what was to become the turbulent 1960s. Near the end of my freshman year, we learned that Lawrence had recruited ten African-American students, to my knowledge the college's first non-white students, who would enter the school the following fall. This seemed very exciting and right to everyone I knew as we realized how narrow and bland our worlds had been. It seemed that we all felt a strong and natural delight in difference and were excited at the prospect of sharing life with more of the many shades and faces of humanity. However, we then also learned that none of these entering freshmen would be able to join Greek life on campus because, according to national policies, these organizations were all segregated.

This was my first recognition of the white privilege I had always enjoyed—indeed, taken for granted—my first realization that so many people in my country lived in a very different reality. Most of my friends were horrified, too, but we quickly found ourselves helpless to change national policies at the local level. Several of us in my sorority wrote letters to our national organization, but to no avail. Then along came finals, the end of the school year, and my return home to Minneapolis for the summer.

About two weeks into my sophomore year back at Lawrence, I became quite sick. Although the school nurse's advice was simple, "Take a couple of aspirins and have a nap before your next class," I was afraid from the symptoms that nephritis had returned, so I went to see a local doctor. It turned out I had hepatitis and mononucleosis. My parents had to come get me and all my belongings and take me back to a Minneapolis hospital. There I was placed in an isolation room for several weeks, where I had hours on end alone. Then I had to recuperate at home for several months more. It was like a repeat of my seventh-grade year.

How does a young person cope with so much solitude and inactivity? I read, of course, whenever I felt able to do so. I also remember trying to quiet my mind by gazing out the window at the natural world or the night sky, but I knew nothing then about centering or meditation practices. And I tried to pray, although I knew little about that, either. Reflecting on those months now, I would say that as one relaxes more and more into slowed-down time, maybe even into the present moment, everything becomes more peaceful somehow. One can enter a state of "flow." I would also say that guidance arises step by step and inner resources rally when sought and expected, trusted. I've never had another one of these extended illnesses, but I did eventually learn to cultivate flow and to build solitary quiet days and retreat times into my life in order to replenish my inner resources, practices desperately needed in today's world.

For many reasons, including course options, convenience, and rising tuition rates not covered by scholarships, I never returned to

Lawrence. Instead I transferred to the University of Minnesota in Minneapolis, which offered a plethora of options and was on the quarter system so I could start in January.

I had always been torn between the pursuit of science versus the liberal arts. In choosing Lawrence, I had clearly been leaning toward the latter. At the U, I took an interdisciplinary humanities course and loved it so much that although my parents wanted me to go into teaching or nursing—the only two careers that seemed safe and possible for young women like me at the time—I chose humanities as my major and gave myself fully to the liberal arts. That particular major was like having five minors—English, history, art or music history, social studies, and a foreign language—plus all the humanities courses available. To me, it offered the incredible opportunity of learning about the sweep of human history and culture. I thought that understanding more fully how we got to where we are would provide clues as to how to live more wisely into the future. It was the kind of quest that has driven me ever since and that underlies my passion in writing this book.

At that time, courses on history and culture in this huge university focused primarily on western civilization. This meant I had extensive exposure to Greek and Roman mythology and philosophy, so I began to appreciate the archetypal dimensions of various gods and goddesses. I did, however, take one class on Russian history and another on the Bible as literature, which offered a whole quarter on the Hebrew scriptures. I loved that course because I learned about the non-dualistic, earthy, and embodied Semitic roots of Christianity. Our professor pointed out emphatically that his was the only course available in the whole university on the Judaic side of the Judeo-Christian heritage, which is every bit as foundational to western civilization, literature, philosophy, art, and so forth as the Greco-Roman heritage.

As for daily life at the U, Theta, my sorority, had a house on campus with a parking lot I could use because I was a sister from another school. That was a huge perk on this rambling campus, especially during Minnesota's blistering winter weather. Other than using the parking lot and meeting some of the women, though, my involvement with the sorority was minimal—until some months later when the chapter president, Anne, became pregnant and left to get married. A short time after her announcement, several of the chapter officers asked to meet with me and said, "Judy, we would like you to consider becoming chapter president for the completion of Anne's term and for the following year."

I stammered something like, "Me? But…why? I-I'm so new! You hardly know me…and I've never served any office here at all."

"We've considered everyone," they said, "and we've all decided that you would be the best person for this role. Plus, you know, it comes with free room and board here at the house, so don't worry, you'll be around and able to learn all you need to know to do the job."

I've since thought that perhaps their choice of me had to do with the fact that, because I was new, I hadn't caused any issues yet and wasn't part of any particular clique. Also, I was a good student, so supposedly keeping up with my studies while taking on the extra responsibilities wouldn't be a problem. In any case, after much thought and discussion with my parents, I finally accepted the role and quite happily moved onto campus.

One result of becoming president of my chapter was that in my junior year I was a delegate to the sorority's national convention. This gave me the opportunity to act on my relatively nascent commitment to try to diversify the organization. I was able to join with several officers from other chapters in pressing the case for our desegregation. It was significant and meaningful work involving many letters and petitions, but we seemed to get nowhere. Once I graduated from college, I ceased all connection with Kappa Alpha Theta and that whole subculture. Now, however, fifty-plus years later, my mixed-race granddaughter has joined, and loves, a wonderfully diverse and very charity-oriented sorority at the University of Southern Maine, Alpha Xi Delta.

Along with my involvement in Greek life, I studied a lot, worked part-time at the campus library, joined a Young Life leadership training program, and enjoyed the drama of football games at this Big Ten school. In fact, from early spring of my junior year to late fall of my senior year, I was in a serious relationship with the star fullback—until I found out that he had gone back to his old girlfriend and was probably getting engaged to her. I was devastated because I cared deeply for him—to the extent that I had seriously wondered if he was The One. But I pulled myself together enough to finish the fall quarter before trying to grapple with my grief. When I had an afternoon alone back home, I sat down with my Bible so I could search for a passage that might speak to me. I allowed myself to drop into my sadness and sense of loss, to enter that liminal space where healing is possible—crying and reading and seeking to be open to what might come.

After a few hours, I came across the First Thessalonians 5:18 passage that reads, "In all things give thanks." It jumped out at me as I realized that deep down, under my grief, there was a sense of rock-solid gratitude and peace, of *Presence*, not unlike the sense I had in that earlier experience of awakening to meaning. I felt I was being held in love and would be okay. Thanksgiving bubbled up and fear dissipated, even though the pain of loss was still there, still fresh. This experience of an inner grounding was powerful enough to hold the paradox of both grief and gratitude at the same time. It gave me the strength to say no when, a month or two later, this same guy sought me out to talk and then asked me on a date, even though he was still somewhat involved with his old girlfriend. Later still, when I met the man I would marry, I was not afraid to love him and commit to a long-distance relationship because I trusted that whatever happened I would be all right. I had come to believe and artic-ulate to myself at a deep level that *life is relationships*, so they are worth everything.

This was, of course, a relatively trivial loss in the context of true human suffering. Many losses make normal functioning impossible for a time, while others rip apart the very fabric of one's being and leave it in shreds. I am in awe of what countless people in the world today must go through simply to survive. My experience did, how-ever, teach me something about grace, about where to go *in myself* in times of trouble, and that has been freeing. It has grounded and guided me through all the losses I've since faced.

Participation in the Young Life leadership training program through-out my time at the U proved so enriching that early in my senior year I decided to apply to become a full-time girl staff leader upon grad-uation. My parents, however, had become increasingly leery of my extensive involvement with Young Life because they thought that, as a college senior with an excellent record, I should be exploring a wide range of career options that might offer good pay, benefits, and opportunities for advancement. So, with some fear and trepidation, I set a date to go home one weekend and break the news of my decision to them.

My folks had been going through a very trying time. Dad had been out of work for several months because an ambitious business venture had fallen through, so he was looking for a new job—no simple thing for a man in his mid-fifties. Therefore I wasn't too surprised when, upon sitting down together on the appointed weekend, Dad said that I had to wait until he told me their news first.

Teary-eyed, he began, "You knew I was in New York a few weeks ago for a job interview, right? On the way home, the flight was grounded in Pittsburgh because of some mechanical issues, so I had a long dinner with my seatmate, a man named Chuck Werley. Do you know him? He's on the Young Life Committee in St. Paul."

"No, I don't think so, Dad," I replied.

He continued, "Over dinner I told Chuck what was going on and why I had been in New York. He could tell how upset and worried I was, so he told me all about his faith in Jesus and then invited me to turn my life over to Him, too. He said I would then enter a whole new journey as a Christian and always be able to trust God for guidance and protection. I realized, Jude, that I had never done that, never understood or thought about it, really. So I said yes and gave my life to Jesus on the spot. I've been meeting with Chuck and studying my Bible with him ever since."

"Wow," I said, mouth agape. "That's…that's just amazing news, Dad." Then I turned to Mom and, seeing tears in her eyes, too, asked, "Mom, what about you in all this?"

"After Dad told me everything that had happened to him," she responded, "I wanted to meet this Chuck, so we invited the Werleys over for dinner. They told us a bit about their story and shared their Christian faith with me. I realized that what they were describing was like what happened with you, and that Dad was different in a way that I wanted, so I committed my life, too. Now we're hunting for a good church and praying together, and…it's been wonderful!"

"My gosh," I managed to say, "this is all the best and most unexpected news ever. I…I hardly know what to say…but I'm very happy for you both. Well…my news is just that I've decided to go on the Young Life staff once I graduate."

"Oh, Judy, that's fantastic!" they exclaimed. "We thought you might decide to do that, and we're totally supportive!"

What an amazingly synchronistic affirmation of my decision that whole encounter was. And what a shift it led to in my relationship with my parents because they now understood the significance to me of my spiritual journey. In fact, they began to view me almost as a spiritual mentor because I had been on the Christian path for so many years.

Although I had begun college as an intensely curious but somewhat angst-filled and needy adolescent, I was definitely growing up. But my problems with food also grew. I had been an eating disorder waiting to happen ever since I had been inducted into the cult of sweets many years earlier by my grandparents and adoring aunt, all of whom at some level equated love and pleasure with food. Also, I became a true product of the cult of thinness that emerged in the sixties with the British supermodel Twiggy. Hollywood's portrayals of female beauty only added to the problem.

For me, things began getting bad when I lived at the sorority house. Many of us had terrible eating habits—overdoing it on sweets or salty snacks, binging on our favorite foods, crash-dieting for special occasions, even stealing food from each other's stashes. Thank God I didn't know anyone who used vomiting to deal with an eating binge or I would undoubtedly have tried that and probably gotten hooked on it. I settled into a binge-eating/crash-dieting pattern that lasted for years and years to one degree or another as I lost and regained the same thirty or so pounds over and over again. I tried every diet that came along, beyond count at this point, including some crazy ones. Once, several years out of college, I stopped eating altogether for about ten days!

All the while, I felt guilt and shame beyond words for the whole pattern. Such is the inner life of the addict. It took me to my knees times without number as I grew spiritually and deepened in self-understanding on many other fronts, but continually failed on this one. In retrospect, I attribute the angst to my pursuit of unrealistic cultural norms of thinness combined with many unresolved psychological needs, which I met with the short-lived comfort of binge eating followed by the self-punishing consolation of a strict diet plan. It took years for me to unpack these issues and more years to learn what constituted healthy eating for my particular body. It wasn't really until my late fifties that I stabilized into healthy eating patterns and began losing weight slowly and naturally. And it wasn't until my mid-sixties that I settled into my body as it seems meant to be—tall and somewhat large-boned, but relatively thin, healthy, and balanced overall. After so long, I am delighted now to feel at ease in my clothes and at home in myself, albeit still paying careful, loving attention to what I eat.

The hierarchy of addictions places eating disorders low on the scale as a trivial matter compared with alcohol, drug, or opioid addictions. The common belief is that someone overweight just needs more nutritional education or better self-discipline. These days, however, with the obesity epidemic so widespread in this country and spreading globally, the seriousness of issues of diet and healthy eating, as well as their connections with both poverty and abuse, is more widely recognized. But solutions are few and far between, and obese people still face discrimination on almost every front.

Given my history, this epidemic is to me a great heartache, and I see it everywhere in Maine. The whole problem is intertwined in this country with the cult of beauty, with our impossible standards of thinness, with the consumerism that tells us we deserve a break today, with the widespread poverty that makes food one of the few rewards many people can afford, with global food conglomerates that profit from the promotion of junk food, and, maybe especially, with our dysfunctional health care system that focuses on treatment rather than prevention because the former is more profitable. These causes are so omnipresent that, as a professor of mine once said about it all, "Being born female in this country is reason enough to develop an eating disorder!"

I recognize that I am grossly oversimplifying a complex problem here, but coming to grips with it personally has been a crucial component of my own awakenings over the years. I am drawn to the Eris archetype in part because she demonstrates the interconnections of beauty, competition, and violence. Remember that in the most familiar Eris story, she is the only Olympian not invited by Zeus to a wedding banquet, presumably because of her reputation as a troublemaker. So she comes uninvited and disrupts everything by throwing out a golden apple "for the fairest." To settle the resulting squabble between three powerful goddesses, Zeus designates Paris as judge. Each of the three then offers him a bribe. In this battle among goddesses for the title of most beautiful, Paris opts for the prize of the most beautiful woman of the time, who also happens to be married—hence the Trojan War. It is important to note that Eris's actions didn't so much cause the war as illuminate its roots in greed and self-interest. These dynamics of inclusion–exclusion, unhealthy competition, power plays, and the cult of beauty still reign. The Eris archetype demands that we wake up to their death-dealing toll and evolve.

Chapter 5

Meeting My True Love

About the time I was to graduate from the U, the current Young
Life staff woman in Minneapolis left to get married, so there
was an opening and I was hired. That summer, I was sent to a staff
training program in Colorado. For much of June and July, I stayed
at Frontier Ranch, the Young Life camp I had attended years before,
to learn the ropes of the ministry's counseling component. Then, for
the month of August, I attended the Young Life Institute, a gradu-
ate-level theological degree program for staff held on the grounds of
a private school in Colorado Springs. Dynamic and wonderful seminary professors and their families from around the country lived
there with us for the month and taught courses. It was an amazing summer, but the most significant and life-changing event was
that I met Jack Carpenter, a Young Life staff person from Fairfield
County, Connecticut.

Jack was at Frontier for a week with kids from his club. I first
noticed him one night when he was up front leading the singing—a
blond, athletic-looking guy of average height with a very warm and
engaging smile. *Such a cutie,* I thought, *with such a great voice…and
so charismatic and funny!* I later learned that I had been pointed out
to him by one of the leaders I knew, so, to my delight, he began flirt-
ing with me whenever our paths crossed. For the most part, these
were just short conversations or maybe a shared laugh or an inviting comment—"I'll see you there"—accompanied by his sparkling
blue eyes and fantastic smile. I was particularly thrilled when he

complimented me at the final banquet: "You look great tonight…in fact, you are gorgeous!" By then we had discovered that we were going to be together again in August at the Young Life Institute, so these flirtations took on more meaning. I began thinking that this budding relationship might have a chance to go somewhere despite the fact that we lived halfway across the country from each other. Clearly I was quite smitten, and I certainly believed the feeling was mutual—until Jack went back to Connecticut and I overheard some women talking about him one night in the Tuwashie, the girls'/women's communal bathroom.

"Do you know that Jack Carpenter from Connecticut? I certainly enjoyed hanging out with him!"

"Yup, I do know him, but I thought he was paying a lot of attention to *me*!"

Then from a different voice, "You both should know that he gets involved with a different woman every summer!"

I was furious, mostly at myself for having been taken in, but also at Jack for being so superficial and fickle. Consequently, once we got to the Institute, I studiously avoided him, looking in the other direction when he was around and ignoring his efforts to engage me in conversation. Despite these snubs, he remained his warm and engaging, somewhat flirtatious self. This went on for several days until dinnertime one evening. Jack had just returned from a trip to Frontier Ranch and told me, quite publicly, that a girl from my club who was there on work crew made him promise to "Give Judy a kiss from me when you get back." Now, this girl knew perfectly well that I had a crush on Jack, so she was clearly conniving to connect us. But Jack was so teasingly cute about the request and got so many people involved that I eventually stopped trying to ignore him and broke down laughing. Then one of our professors, Dr. Jim Martin of Princeton Theological Seminary, entered in on the fun and sealed the deal by daring me to let Jack fulfill his promise by kissing me out on the front steps of the dining center.

The rest, as they say, is history. Jack and I soon discovered that, not only were we attracted to each other, but we loved being together and could talk for hours on end about almost everything. It was quite a month: I came alive to the material I was studying, learned a lot, and fell in love!

One of the things I learned was that Christianity has an extremely conservative, fundamentalist side. Jack and his brother Reid, who was also there at the Institute that month, had grown up in a subculture in which everything was about personal salvation from damnation through faith in Jesus, accompanied by a narrow moral code of conduct. In their family and church, activities like dancing, smoking, drinking alcohol, going to movie theaters, playing cards, and doing much beyond going to church on Sundays were forbidden. Jack and Reid were on the way to extricating themselves from this strictness. In fact, I learned a lot about it while sneaking cigarettes with Reid out back in the woods. But I had never heard of this kind of thing before. It certainly hadn't come up in my prior experience of Christianity or Young Life.

To me the big questions one's Christian faith ought to address had to do with suffering in the world—prejudice, poverty, injustice, oppression, war—not with such mundane personal matters as whether or not I went dancing. In Jack's upbringing, the one big question was about being saved from hellfire and damnation through faith in Jesus, which should be demonstrated through these moral behaviors—a totally opposite orientation.

We did, however, share the fairly common Christian belief that sex outside of marriage was wrong, so it was several years before I told Jack that I had been sexually active in high school. I had to come to the point where my shame about this history was overshadowed by my guilt at not having been truthful with him. When I finally confessed it all, after tearfully saying we had to talk because I had something awful to tell him, he actually sighed in relief. "Oh, honey," he said, "I forgive you. You were so upset and sad that I was afraid you were going to tell me that you were in love with someone else or didn't want to be married anymore or something. Those high school years were a long time ago and they don't need to matter anymore."

This loving and compassionate response went a long way toward helping me forgive myself. It also further steeled my resolve to break the habit of letting little or big lies slip out when I felt threatened or insecure, a habit begun in childhood with "David did that, not me," or "He's the one who started it," or "That's not my fault, I wasn't even here!" I know now that it is far better to stop myself or fess up early on than to carry even low-grade lies for any length of time—unless, of course, they are intentional lies for the protection of someone else.

Jack and I have looked at the polarity in our background stories—between his fear of death and damnation and my search for meaning in life—countless times together over the years, starting that first summer with a New Testament course Jack had previously taken. The professor, Dr. Jim Martin of the "kiss dare," challenged us all to open up to the fullness of Jesus's life and message: his focus on mercy, justice, love, and service on behalf of the poor and oppressed everywhere. Jesus broke all the norms by eating with sinners and outcasts. Everyone was welcome at his table! This was the Good News or gospel that Young Life needed to spread, according to Dr. Martin, instead of a simplistic message of personal salvation. I loved his perspective because I believed so passionately that many young people were, like me, hungry for a broad gospel message that would give meaning and purpose to their lives for the long haul.

Dr. Martin also inadvertently presented us with our first big challenge. Jack and I had begun spending way too much time behind the gym together, making out instead of studying, so we were both very worried about how I would do on Dr. Martin's notoriously difficult midterm exam. Jack didn't want me to have the embarrassment of failing, nor did he want to suffer his own embarrassment about it, I'm sure. I hadn't told him that I had been high school valedictorian and elected to Phi Beta Kappa in college because it hadn't seemed necessary or relevant. So after the exam, Jack nervously asked Dr. Martin how I had done. He was told, "She wrote the finest exam I've ever read in all my years of teaching!" Dr. Martin also told Jack that he had learned that I was in Phi Beta Kappa.

This was all way too much for Jack, who felt I hadn't been honest with him. And it was too much for all the other guys, apparently, because they told him in no uncertain terms, "You don't want a woman who's smarter than you are!"

I was horrified. Here was the whole pedestal issue again. It was dangerous for a woman to be singled out for any natural abilities other than being beautiful, although that certainly held its own dangers! I remember trying to explain to Jack, "Honey, this academic stuff is just something I seem able to do, but it's not the real me.

It doesn't have anything to do with my deeper self and all the things we talk about together. You know I'm not a scary person, and I don't ever want to seem scary to you."

Jack relaxed gradually as the power of our connection outweighed his fears, but I did not yet understand what I was doing to myself by denying my gifts, my full personhood. How often, I wonder, do women do something like this to themselves in order to placate the fears of some insecure man? How often do they silence themselves in order not to appear threatening to the men in power around them? How often do they do it because their very lives would be in danger if they challenged the patriarchal status quo? And how often are they belittled, maligned, attacked, tortured, raped, even killed, if they do dare to give voice to their truth. This is all so horrifying that…words fail me! It is a tragedy beyond words! Our world *desperately* needs the full power, insight, wisdom, truth, and authority of every single woman! We need archetypes like Eris to inspire us to speak truth to power and become women warriors for justice.

Dr. Martin became a close friend of ours that summer. We stayed in touch and even visited him occasionally over the years that followed. Through our many conversations and his biblical scholarship, Jack and I soon embraced, privately at least, a form of Christian universalism that resonated with my own sense of God. Jesus's life, death, and resurrection serve everyone because the love of God—which is stronger than death—embraces the whole created order, including *all people* regardless of whether or not they profess the name of Jesus or are even part of some religious tradition.

When Jack and I finished Institute that summer of '63, he came home to Minneapolis with me to meet my family and to give us time together away from the fishbowl of Institute life. My parents both adored him from the moment they met him. Sadly, my mom, true to form though probably kidding a bit, even asked him what he saw in me. Jack's five-day visit proved to be quite memorable—complete with me falling from a horse while riding double bare-back with Jack, breaking my arm, and ending up in the hospital—and it launched our developing relationship to a whole new level.

One surprising connection we discovered between Jack and my folks was that Jack's dear friend and Young Life committee chairman, Bart Swift, had come to Christianity through an encounter on a grounded airline flight with a man from St. Paul, Chuck Werley, the same man my dad had encountered under the same circumstances. This is just one example of the synchronicities, synergies, serendipities that any one of us might see when we seek to be reflective. Whereas I've noticed many throughout my life, I had no idea there were so many of such significance that they would make their way into a book like this. I'm newly encouraged to *pay attention*. Our lives are held in unimaginable, often delightful, interconnected webs of meaning.

After his visit, Jack and I entered into a long-distance courtship: writing daily letters, speaking often on the phone, and making as many red-eye, cheap flights between Minneapolis and New York as we could manage until our marriage almost two years later. Those years were both intensely romantic and deeply scary for me because I so wanted this relationship to work but was so insecure about being lovable. I also feared I might go in some directions spiritually that would end up leading us apart. For example, there was a lot of emphasis in Christian circles around me at the time on the "fullness of the Holy Spirit," and my natural curiosity drew me to learn more about it. But what would Jack think? Might this exploration seem too "far-out" to him with his more conservative background? Blessedly, though, whenever we were together again, we found that our paths still converged. Following my curiosity, not my fear, actually drew us together—a great lesson in trusting my interests and my heart.

Serving on the Young Life staff for those two years, I quickly discovered that I loved many aspects of the work but dreaded others. My favorite times were the weekly visioning, brainstorming, theologizing sessions we had with all the staff together, sessions at which, I realize in retrospect, I was the only woman present. I also loved meeting individually with women or college student volunteers and leading the small group Bible studies with girls from various clubs. But the more extroverted demands of outreach to young people at a school or at games and other events, were very difficult for me—quite outside my introverted comfort zone. And my responsibilities that August at Castaway, Young Life's newest camp in Detroit Lakes, Minnesota, where I was the only staff woman present and on duty for everything, were *way* outside my comfort zone.

Throughout my time on staff, but especially that summer at Castaway, I couldn't wait to be married, move to Connecticut, and leave my former life behind. I secretly wished I would be leaving my difficulties with food behind, too. It took some years for me to understand the cost to women of leaving behind their own world for their man's—and for me to grasp all the unfinished work I had yet to do in relation to my family story and personal issues.

Jack's own set of fears became focused on the idea of marriage itself. According to his narrow Christian upbringing, the husband is the head of the household and therefore responsible not only for the success of the marriage, but also for the faith journeys of his wife and children. Since Jack is fundamentally a very loyal and responsible person, and since several of his friends were already unhappy in their marriages, the whole prospect began to seem more and more like a huge burden to him—and way too scary. We talked about this several times until one day, in total exasperation and quite unlike myself, I said, "Well, you ought to marry me, then, because I know my marriage will work out!" Almost immediately, I began backpedaling and explaining that I only meant I trusted it would work out because I didn't want any marriage that wasn't "of God." Months later I learned that my impetuous claim had helped Jack view marriage as a partnership instead of just a responsibility. So he began planning a surprise marriage proposal at lovely Kent Falls in Kent, Connecticut, for my September visit.

We rode to Kent Falls on Jack's motorcycle, an adventure in itself. He told me that the place was a childhood favorite where they used to dive into a pool to look for coins people had wished upon. It was a gorgeous sunny but very cold day. Jack, however, told me he had on his swimsuit so that he could dive for any treasures we might spot. Once we had climbed to the pool, he pointed out a tiny shimmering object in the water. I stood trembling on a ledge in my winter jacket as he disrobed and jumped into the freezing water. He swam a few strokes, went down and came up with something in his hand.

"What is it?" I called.

He looked down and answered, "A dime!"

I said, "Cool," or something like that.

But Jack said, "I'm going back down to see if I can't find something more special."

This time when he came up, he waded back to me, trembling violently from the cold (and the drama) and then held out his hand—in which lay a diamond ring! I was overwhelmed, shocked, scared Jack might have a stroke or worse from the cold—and *so* happy. I said *Yes!* of course and quickly got him out of the water. Then I learned that his cousin, John David Borgman, had arrived that morning to place the ring in the pool and was up above us in the woods taking pictures—priceless images which sadly, years later, a dog destroyed.

We eventually learned from his cousin that the ring hadn't shown up as well as the dime with which they had practiced, so he put a dime under the ring. Jack apparently knocked the ring off the dime when he went down the first time. What a miracle that he found it on his second try! And what a romantic and adventurous engagement it was, if a bit risky. Jack had once promised me that he would "make every day an adventure," and this was quite a beginning!

Jack and I were married on June 5, 1965, and launched into life together on the proverbial shoestring, beginning with me wearing a borrowed wedding dress and us having our wedding reception in the church parlor. I was quite anxious leading up to the wedding because I felt like a most imperfect bride in many ways. That is not surprising, given my early mother story and her take on my many imperfections, particularly that I was *unloving*. I knew that my love for Jack was somewhat fearful and that such love could drive a person away. This led me to think a lot about the passage in I John: "Perfect love casts out fear." I knew that only the Spirit could perfect love, so I prayerfully sought to turn all my love for Jack over to God so that it could flow back to him free of fear. This proved to be such a meaningful practice that I have continued it throughout my life whenever I become aware of being fearful in a relationship or situation, to the point that it is often, blessedly, somewhat automatic—although never simple.

I also, of course, felt anxious and inadequate before the wedding because I hadn't lost the weight I'd wanted to lose. Fortunately, one of my wise bridesmaids, who knew what was going on, said to me, "Jude, no one is perfect! You and Jack will both have lots to work on over the years, and that's how it's meant to be. In fact, it will be bonding to do that work together." Her wise words offered enough consolation that I was thrilled, although quite overwhelmed by the wonder of it all, on our big day.

Right after the wedding, Jack and I took off for his summer assignment in Colorado. During the first semester, he took comprehensive exams at the Institute to complete his master's degree. For the month of August, he was program director at Star Ranch, the Young Life camp in Colorado Springs. Meanwhile, to earn money, I took a job as a waitress at a pancake house for breakfast and dinner shifts. In retrospect, this was a most stressful and foolhardy way to start a marriage, and it almost did us in! We never went to bed or got up at the same times and hardly ever saw each other. When we did, I was sad, lonely, and exhausted while Jack was preoccupied and over his head with responsibilities. He would say, "It will be different when we get back home." But I would say, "How do you know? You've never been married before! We're barely into our marriage, and already you hardly know I'm here!" Fortunately, we were eventually rescued by a wise intervention. One of my bridesmaids visited the camp, met with me, and then quickly told Jack that he'd better start paying attention because I was practically suicidal. He made a noble effort, and we survived. At the end of August, we left Colorado for what proved to be a fresh beginning. In those three months, we had come through the worst of what often takes the entire first year of marriage.

Jack and I began and have remained the best of friends despite our differences, which are many. We have often been saved by our sense of humor, although more than a few times when enraged about something, I would say, in effect, "I know this is funny and we'll laugh about it someday, but don't you dare laugh now!" And of course, many times Jack didn't want to be laughed at, either. But friendship and that shared sense of humor, as well as our mutual and ever-deepening spiritual journeys, have provided great footings for our marriage.

As for our differences, Jack is friendly and socially extroverted, while I am hopefully warm but introverted. I love reading, learning, stretching my mind, and getting into deep conversations. He enjoys a certain amount of that, but generally loves engaging with people in all kinds of circumstances. After all these years, he is still primarily committed to an outreach ministry with young people. One of his richest loves is jazz. Jack grew up seeing the early jazz greats like Bill Evans, Miles Davis, and Dizzy Gillespie live in New York City, and listening to jazz still offers him access to spiritual and bodily ecstasy. He plays trumpet and flugelhorn by ear and has a gorgeous singing voice, while I can't carry a tune unless I'm next to a strong singer. I can't even hear what Jack hears in the dense chords that thrill him most, so music is rarely something we can truly share. However, we have learned over time and with much work that we can honor and delight in each other's gifts without feeling "lesser than."

Chapter 6

Creating a Mixed-Race Family

Back in Darien, Connecticut, Jack and I set up house in a sweet little rental cottage. I did a lot of substitute teaching with junior and senior high schoolers and helped Jack in club, working with several of the girls. We attended a little Congregational Church in North Greenwich, where we developed several long-lasting friendships. Then, late the following summer, I got pregnant. What a mysterious, marvelous, scary, all-encompassing transformation that is for a woman. Our beloved first child, Amy, was born in May 1967. Within months, I was pregnant again, and dear son Josh was born in July 1968. My hands were suddenly and wonderfully very full, and it became almost impossible to continue sharing ministry with Jack. I was a happy new mom!

We did, though, share what Jack called Work-Study Trips with our Young Life students. Along with other leaders and our children, we took these wealthy young people on summer service projects where they worked hard and shared life with people living in impoverished areas such as Sunset Gap in the Appalachian Mountains of Tennessee. We also went to Koinonia Farm in Americus, Georgia, the creative community that spawned Habitat for Humanity. It was started by theologian Clarence Jordan, author of the *Cotton Patch Version*, a paraphrase in local dialect of the New Testament that was published right around that time. We occasionally had the incredible privilege of sitting at Clarence's feet while he shared his newest thoughts. What life-changing opportunities these trips were for each and every one of us, awakening us to the polarities of privilege and poverty built into the class system in which we were so thoroughly embedded. A few students returned to Koinonia to be part of the community after school, and at least one, who is still a close friend, met his wife there. Several have gone on to help out with Habitat for Humanity in various settings. There are not many experiences as growth-producing as intentionally stepping out of your familiar life into a relatively safe learning environment where you give yourself in intensive labor for the needs of others—particularly when you can get to know and respect those *others* as simply fellow human beings.

Jack and I also established rich connections in the little neighborhood of row houses in Stamford, Connecticut, where we moved a month after Josh was born—with help on the down payment from Jack's parents. It was inexpensive enough that one of his cousins, a teacher, moved in behind us, and one of his oldest friends and Josh's godfather, also a teacher, moved in next door. We all frequently shared child care, meals, celebrations, and down times, as well as the spiritually motivated intention to care for our other neighbors.

These years brought many blessings. There were times of insight and inner growth through reading a wide range of material as well as times of inner peace and guidance when struggling and praying through some difficulty. Such experiences, along with Jack's love and a sense of community, left me feeling more acceptable, more healed, although I had a long way to go. Ah, we wounded human creatures, so immersed in this materialistic, competitive culture and so separated from our spiritual souls and ground. It takes a lifetime of inner work to become whole. The alternative is unthinkable to me, though, and death-dealing all around.

Meanwhile, these were the sixties, dynamic times indeed with assassinations, race riots, marches, everything—including hippie communes and the Jesus, Black Power, and women's movements. Jack and I cared passionately about it all and communed with those of like minds, but our family and work life demanded most of our time and energy. I had become the stay-at-home mom hanging out diapers in the backyard that I had foreseen in my youthful years of searching with Toni. I loved Jack and my children and would not have missed out on them for the world. Furthermore, I had the world of books and many opportunities for stimulating conversations, plus conferences or other events to attend with Jack. But I definitely became bored over time and probably more than a bit depressed.

This was particularly apparent to me during Jack's month-long summer-camp assignments at Saranac Village, Young Life's large rustic lakeside facility in the gorgeous Adirondacks. We all accompanied him there and lived in the building that housed the staff and their families. That month was heaven for our children. They had other young kids to play with and the run of the camp, including access to all its amenities and the entertainment parts of the high school campers' program. The magic of the north woods, accompanied by the yummy smells of wood smoke and hot chocolate, got imprinted in their hearts and memories.

But I struggled. After the first year, Jack was always the camp manager and so busy and preoccupied with his many responsibilities that, as in our early marriage camp experience, he hardly knew I was there. He would literally walk by me on some path and never see or acknowledge me. Whole meals might pass without his turning once to talk to me because he was caught up in camp business with someone else. But the worst times were the obligatory weekly middle-of-the-night fire drills, which were up to him to schedule—without, by law, alerting *anyone*. When the alarm went off, he had to rush straight to his command post, while I had to get our kids up (four, eventually) and haul them way down to the beach, which was at the very farthest point on the camp property from the staff house.

Although none of the wives liked fire-alarm nights, I seemed to be the only one among us who was bored and frustrated by the whole setup. However, I tried really hard not to burden Jack with that fact because there was absolutely nothing he could do about it. Nor did I feel I could confide in the other wives, who were happily enjoying what seemed to be their favorite month of the year. They loved the fellowship and camaraderie, the distractions that kept their children occupied and happy, the shared participation in all kinds of handicrafts, and the freedom from any responsibilities for meals. I enjoyed all that, too, but I couldn't seem to enjoy it twenty-four/seven for a whole month year after year. I did allow myself to pull away and read in my room for stretches of time, but it felt odd to be the only one doing that—like there was something wrong with me. One summer,

I remember burying myself in handiwork for so many hours that I couldn't stand to pick up knitting or sewing for over a year.

All in all, these were hard years for me. Huge parts of me were not being fed, and this affected not only my parenting abilities, but all aspects of my life. I wonder now how many women, for how many generations, in how many countries in the world have struggled and are still struggling with living half a life? How many are so constrained by their culture's rules and mores, or simply by responsibilities and poverty, that they are unable to express and develop their gifts? What would our world be like if this were not the case? And what could our world become if women globally were set free to be their whole selves? These are some of my dreams and the dreams of countless women, as well as of many wise and compassionate men, in our times. They are the dreams that inspire me to champion the dark feminine, warrior-for-justice archetype of Eris in hopes of turning the tide of patriarchal power and capitalistic greed—in hopes, ultimately, of securing planetary survival.

Long before I fully saw and understood much of this, we expanded our family. At the end of the sixties and for most of the early seventies, we were part of a committed group of nine couples, including our two close neighbors in the row houses. The group began with the men meeting together weekly as a mission community to deal with issues around the local Young Life ministry, as well as such sixties lifestyle questions as seeking economic justice, serving the poor, and living more simply.

Then we wives decided to get babysitters so we could meet together ourselves instead of sitting home alone. We already knew one another fairly well so were more than ready to share deeply. First, though, we set some ground rules: "Let's make sure everyone gets her time, and that we really listen to whoever is speaking."

"Absolutely, but let's always begin by going around the circle and hearing a little bit from each one so we know if anyone has something big going on."

"And if someone does, maybe she can have the whole session."

"That sounds right...I'm thinking, though, that we're really going to have to discipline ourselves so we don't just fritter away our time chatting."

"Absolutely. But, you know, if we do this thoughtfully and carefully enough, over time we should be able to hear all about each other's families and marriage issues…and also how we're each feeling about all the stuff going on in the world right now."

Before long, our conversations became so much richer and deeper than the men's that they asked if we could please all meet together. We did so then for several years, sharing personal stories, delving into all the hot topics of the day, and exploring options for more communal and just living, a dominant theme in that tumultuous era. We were a typical sixties "encounter group," facing right into all our personal and interpersonal issues, including the challenges of our very different levels of financial privilege. We were exploring how to live a smaller version of what we wanted for the community at large and for the world.

At one point within the group, Jack turned to me and, with a twinkle in his eye, asked, "Mrs. Carpenter, what's coming next for your family—more children or some other kind of work or service?" This question was totally out of the blue. There must have been a lull in the conversation, and he must have been thinking about this for himself. In any case, he put me and the topic of our family life right onto the hot seat.

I exclaimed, "Jack!" but everyone was looking at us expectantly, so I sighed and proceeded to explain some of our thoughts to the group. "We've always kind of agreed we'd like four kids. Jack wants more than the two in his family, and I don't want the imbalance of three, like my family. But here we are with two already, a girl and a boy, and we're all so conscious of the need for zero population growth because of overpopulation globally that…we're kind of stuck. We've thought a little about adoption, but…never seriously discussed it."

This launched the group into the subject of adoption. We all knew people who had followed that route, some because they couldn't have children and several because they wanted more children but were committed to zero population growth, including some close Young Life friends who had adopted mixed-race kids. By the end of what was kind of a rambling discussion, Jack and I realized that in order to think this through, we needed to find out what adoption entailed and whether or not there were actually children who needed homes but were not likely to be adopted by another family.

So we made an appointment for an interview at an agency in White Plains, New York, that had been recommended to us by close friends, themselves a mixed-race couple who had adopted through the agency and served on its board. There we learned that there were several categories of hard-to-place children, and that homes for them were definitely needed. We already knew that we were most interested in getting a baby, and we quickly realized that we didn't have the financial resources to adopt a physically challenged or overseas child. It also didn't seem right to bring one of the northwest Native American children then available to Fairfield County, Connecticut. Gradually, the category that seemed to make the most sense for us was mixed-race, half-Black children, but the thought of daring to adopt and raise such a child in our white family was incredibly daunting.

After talking and praying about all the options and issues before us, Jack and I finally came to the momentous and far-reaching decision that we wanted more children but did not want our life choices to be governed by fear—our own or that of our parents and extended family. We also believed that we had the kind of ties and strong friendships in the Black community that would support us and our children along the way. Jack had become involved with the Young Life folks working in both the Lower East Side of New York and other cities nationally, plus he was developing mixed-racial, inner-city work locally. So we entered into all the assessments and home studies required by the agency and formally requested a mixed-race baby.

In September 1971, about nine months after we'd begun the process, we were blessed with the arrival in our lives of tiny three-week-old Anna. It was love at first sight for Jack and me, as well as for little Amy and Josh. Our hearts went out to Anna's uniquely adorable and vulnerable little self. We were also moved by compassion for the primal grief—the loss of her birth mother—that she would forever carry no matter what we did.

Serendipitously—miraculously, even—that month a nineteen-year-old Black man, A.G. (Albert George) Miller of Columbia, Missouri, came to live with us for a weekend—but ended up staying the whole school year. He was going to college locally and working with the fledgling urban Young Life club in Stamford. However, the planned student–staff housing didn't come together until the following summer, so A.G. became a friendly bridge builder with all our neighbors, preparing them, and us, to welcome our new baby. A.G. also became, and has remained, a real part of our family and we of his. He is Anna's godfather and the godfather of our second adopted child. (Both children had been born to white mothers and Black fathers, so I could assuage my sense of inadequacy with the thought that their birth mothers would have faced the same shortcomings I did.)

Most importantly, A.G., along with one of his closest friends, also in Stamford preparing for youth ministry, began revealing to Jack and me our layers and layers of unconscious racism. They questioned, challenged, and confronted us, as well as the white and privileged hosts of A.G.'s friend, time and again for hours on end about our beliefs and assumptions, particularly the unconscious assumption by whites at all levels that we "know what's best for Black people." They also took issue with Young Life's focus on white suburban high schools and with the biases and blindness *that* revealed. I can still see them standing before us in our living room—two big, beautiful, and passionate young Black men—gesticulating with clenched fists as they struggled to articulate the realities, the frustrations as well as the blessings, of their lived experience.

Jack and I sat and listened as best we could—the humble, grateful, but fairly overwhelmed recipients of so much we did not know and had not seen. I remember asking lots of questions and trying hard to remember names and grasp the stories about their rich roots in the South and about growing up poor and Black in inner-city Columbia. These guys shared countless frightening, heartbreaking, and enraging experiences of prejudice and injustice. We also learned about the books they were studying by writers like Malcolm X and James Baldwin, books which Jack and I soon began reading for ourselves.

In retrospect, these passionate young Black men were maturing into their own clarity and vision about race and calling, in part through their honest interactions with us and our white naïveté. On our end, we knew it was all a *gift* even as it was happening, but, oh my, it was not easy to be so stretched while we were simultaneously trying to parent our two young children, our new baby, and, to some extent, this young college kid who was living away from home for the first time—and all with just one bathroom in the house!

A.G.'s presence that first year of Anna's life seemed to us a serendipitous seal of approval on the whole daring enterprise of her adoption. So, as he prepared to leave, Jack and I thought a lot about our intention, barring unforeseen difficulties with a first adoption, to adopt a second child so that our family would be more racially balanced. Since from the very beginning Anna had unquestionably fit right into the family, we decided to go ahead and explore the possibilities of getting another child through the same agency.

We soon learned that the children most in need of placement at that point were older children. What a formidable option. Our commitment all along had been to consider a child who might not otherwise find a home. We knew now that we had significant community as well as family support, plus we both had extensive experience working with young people. In retrospect, though, we were simply very, very naïve—both about the issues a child from the foster-care system might have and about what it might mean in the lives of our current children to bring in a new older brother. Had we known, we might not have dared do it, but what an incalculable loss that would have been.

Since Amy and Josh were young enough to think that getting a big brother would be a good thing, and since our paperwork was still current, we soon went ahead and asked for a six- to seven-year-old mixed-race boy. A few months later, after the agency had looked all around for a good option for us, given that they were already invested in our family, we were told about little David. He had been released for adoption at the time of his birth in Binghamton, New York, and since then had been in three different foster families there. He had been with his current family longer than any of their other foster children, so he really needed a good placement. For our part, we had to be certain we would take him before he learned about and met us so that he would not have to face another loss.

Once all was totally discussed, processed, and finally decided, Jack and I drove to Binghamton to meet six-year-old David (whom we baptized John David, the name he has gone by since high school, usually shortened to J.D.). He was a really cute kid, with chocolat-ey-brown skin, darker than Anna's, and big kinky hair compared to her somewhat tight curls. He seemed a little shy but was clearly very curious, and our hearts opened to him right away. We played him a tape the kids had made of some songs and words of welcome and also showed him some of their drawings and several photos of the family.

"This is Amy and Josh, David," Jack explained. "They are five and four years old and can't wait to meet you. They drew these pictures and made this tape for you. This is baby Anna, who is just turning one. We adopted her last year. We are all so excited for you to join our family, too."

He thought a bit and asked, "What does it mean exactly to be adopted?"

"Well," I responded, "when you are adopted it means you become totally part of our family forever. You have our last name, and we take care of you until you are ready to leave home as a man and take care of yourself. It's a lifelong relationship."

He took this in a bit, answered our questions about his cur-rent foster home, and then asked, "Want me to sing you a song they taught me? They always laugh when I sing it."

We said, "Sure, that would be great. We can even tape it to play for the other kids."

So he sang, "Daniel Boone was a man, a big man, but the bear was bigger and he ran like a nigger up a tree!"

After Jack and I gaped at each other in shock at David's inno-cence, we thanked him for singing the song—and wanted more than ever to give him a new home. A month or so later, our little family went to pick him up in the Volkswagen van we had just pur-chased to accommodate our new bigger family. And that confused, dear little guy had to leave behind everything and everybody he knew and come away with us to a whole different life.

That fall, church friends who had moved to Orlando, Florida, gifted us with the incredible family adventure of a week-long trip to visit Disney World. They not only hosted us, they also paid our travel expenses. One afternoon, Jack was sunning himself by their backyard pool and called John David over to sit with him. Our new son replied, "Oh, no. I don't want to get any darker. They shoot them people in the streets!" It was another of many steps in our mutual education.

That same fall, Jack and I made what would later prove to be a very significant decision—to leave our Congregational Church and join the local Episcopal Church, St. Paul's in Darien. Several factors led us to this move, but a main one was that this particular parish was in a dynamic period of renewal and growth, which drew many Black families and people of diverse and difficult circumstances to worship in this otherwise white and wealthy commuter town. Since we did not want our children's experience of Christianity to be all white, we began going there. We loved the liturgy and the powerfully charismatic biblical teaching and preaching offered by Terry Fulham, the rector at that time. I remember being moved to tears Sunday after Sunday as I watched "the halt and the lame" go forward for communion. I felt such compassion for these people and so humbled by my own apparent well-being because I knew they bore on the outside the kind of brokenness and need I carried on the inside.

A year or two later, when classes were offered for people who wanted to be confirmed as Episcopalians, we were interested but found we had a time conflict so couldn't attend. Terry told us that he would be happy to confirm us anyway because he was confident we would learn about the denomination someday. So we became Episcopalians. Jack was then the New York regional director of Young Life, but shortly after the confirmation ceremony, his supervisor said he wanted us to relocate to New Jersey and run the region from there.

In the spring of 1975, on our last Sunday at St. Paul's, Terry invited us to come forward and kneel for a farewell blessing. Then he invited anyone who had been touched by our ministry to come forward and lay hands on us. As we knelt there, we heard this mass movement of people coming from every direction behind us. We then felt the press of countless bodies around us and the weight of their many, many hands, touching us or stretching out to one another if they couldn't reach us. I can't help but wonder to what degree and in what ways that powerful commissioning changed the course of our lives.

We stayed with our commitment to the Episcopal Church following that move to New Jersey and the next move a little over a year later to the Boston area, when Jack became New England regional director. There I went to seminary and was eventually ordained an Episcopal priest, so Terry's prophetic words that I would learn about the denomination someday came startlingly true.

With the addition of John David, our family had become complete. The two adoptions prompted us to learn in our hearts what has recently become a political declaration—*Black Lives Matter!* If our Black baby girl—it was always hard for little Anna to understand why she was considered Black since her skin is actually light brown—and our Black little boy were utterly precious to us, then all such girls and boys are precious, too. If I wanted my adoptive children to be safe in this world as they grow up, then all people like them must be safe. One time, young Amy and Josh told us their friends thought we had adopted Anna and John David to be our slaves or servants, and they weren't sure what to say back. Another time, a neighbor warned us that while he was fine with our kids while they were little, he did not want our son ever to try to date his daughter.

These are relatively mild examples of the pernicious prejudices abounding in our culture and now widely surfacing, having gained a certain amount of political endorsement, even encouragement. To a certain extent, the white power structure has always tolerated—used and abused, really—Black girls and women, but for the most part it has feared and disdained Black males. In subtle ways, as Black mothers have always known, our culture has not intended for these sons to survive! If they do, they are incarcerated whenever possible. Facing the public manifestation of systemic, institutionalized dis-crimination is hard for us white folks to do. It is even harder for us to open up enough to face our internalized racism and begin to deal with it. We conveniently define racism as individual, intentional, and prejudicial *actions*, so we can tell ourselves that we don't do those things. At the same time, we deny our learned reactions to and sub-tle fear of difference, as well as the systemic structures that privilege us and oppress whole categories of people. God help us…

Chapter 7

Becoming a Woman Priest

Even at the time of the adoptions, I had a hunch that adding to our family in such a challenging way was somewhat an attempt on my part to make mothering a big enough job to satisfy my low-grade boredom and hunger at finding myself in that dreaded hanging-diapers role. Initially, blessedly, with each of our four children, I experienced several months of pure joy and gratitude at their arrival into our family, an inner emotional and spiritual affirmation of my motherhood and our decision to adopt. Gradually, though, a hunger returned, hunger being a nuanced word for a woman with an eating disorder. It manifested itself in a sense of restlessness that no amount of housework, handiwork, or even reading could assuage, plus, as always, the temptation to binge eat. I didn't know what to do with myself and realized I was becoming depressed. Furthermore, our children were growing older, and we needed me to get a job to augment our income. It was clearly time to come to grips with what was going on and what work I could do.

After we relocated to a suburb of Trenton, New Jersey, in 1975, part of Jack's work involved supervising the student volunteers from nearby Princeton Theological Seminary, and I happily got involved with these stimulating young people, too. So Jack, recognizing my need to use my mind more fully, urged me to take a course at Princeton. I remember saying, "Jack, ministry's your job, not mine. You're the one who should take a course, not me." Instead I went to work as Jack's secretary. That was a really bad idea! He was too independent and, in my mind, stubborn, to listen to what I as his secretary thought needed to happen. For example, a call would come in for him, I would tell the person that Jack would call back, and then Jack would tell me that he wasn't going to call that person. Thankfully, for some very complicated reasons, Jack was soon reassigned as New England Regional Director and relocated to the Boston area. I would happily be going home to my roots and to where I still had extended family.

In 1976, we bought a home in Newton, a western suburb of Boston. It had a significant Black population, including several mixed-race families on our street. I was delighted by the move because New Jersey had never felt like home to either of us, but once the kids were all in school and the house was arranged to my satisfaction, I had to face the question of what to do with myself. I certainly wasn't going to work for Jack again, but, with my humanities major, I didn't know what work I might be qualified for beyond getting a job at the local supermarket. My low-grade depression increased, so I seriously embarked on a quest to identify my gifts and inner calling.

Several close friends suggested that my richest gifts were in the area of pastoral counseling, the kind of deep work with individuals or groups that I knew I loved. I had always trusted that I could listen well and offer support in the informal pastoral relationships that had come my way. Jack came up with the idea that perhaps I could study clinical pastoral education at Andover Newton Theological School (ANTS) right there in Newton in order to obtain some credentials. Since he was taking a continuing education course there himself, he inquired on my behalf and learned that the only way to take courses on a credentialed career path was to be enrolled in the Master of Divinity degree program. When he told me that, my belly and heart practically leapt out of my body as I thought, *I could study biblical theology!* This is the kind of bodily testimony—an awakening—to an unknown longing that one daren't ignore. Our closest friends all agreed that this seemed right and urged me to go for it.

At this point, I was thirteen years post-college and terrified of taking the Graduate Record Exam (GRE) in order to be accepted into a degree program. That January, all four kids got sick, one after the other, and I was homebound for three solid weeks. I decided there was obviously no way I could go back to school, not to mention find the money for it. But because Jack had made that inquiry in the fall, I received an invitation from ANTS to a February weekend program for prospective students. While Jack watched the kids, I attended and became enthralled by the offerings and the opportunity to engage my heart, mind, and soul in this kind of study. During the course of that weekend, I learned that the perfect background for seminary was considered to be an education in the humanities, my college major—such an affirmation of a choice that had often been called into question by more practical folks! I also learned that, because I had been elected to Phi Beta Kappa, I was exempt from taking the GRE. Although I procrastinated submitting my application until the last moment that spring, ANTS accepted me, and that fall I signed up for one course, Introduction to the Old Testament.

I loved that course and threw myself into it, even as Jack and I tried to sort out how to function as a family with me so involved with classwork and my new school. For my part, I rationalized that it would surely be a good model for the kids to see their mother engaged in serious study. I just asked that they not leave the kitchen a mess and dirty dishes around when they came home from school so I could cook supper without having to clean up first. One wouldn't think that would be such a hard or unreasonable thing to ask. For his part, Jack requested that I let him have meetings or business guests at our home even if I couldn't help out or was in a crunch time at school. This probably shouldn't have been too much to ask either, but it was sure difficult for me and for everyone else to follow through on our promises. I remember once, during exam week, sitting down with Young Life guests to a dinner completely prepared by Jack and being mortified by some of the results. Fortunately, we usually found that we could laugh together later about many such moments as we struggled through this huge shift in roles.

My obvious excitement about school also brought challenges to the marriage itself. Some of our close friends, including two couples from our sixties encounter group, had split up by then, and Jack worried about us. "I'm afraid you're going to go off in some new direction away from the family, Jude. All you seem to care about is what you're learning," he said one time. And another time, "Chances are you're going to meet someone else there at school and decide to leave me and the kids."

I would fervently reply something like, "Oh, honey, I love you and am totally committed to our family. All of this isn't going to take me away. On the contrary, it's going to make it possible for you and me to share life and work more fully than ever in the future!"

Despite many reassurances, though, my obvious excitement outweighed my words and left Jack feeling threatened for the first few years—in retrospect, his midlife crisis years. This vulnerability also had to do with frustrating issues within Young Life and with the relative obscurity of his role compared with the status conferred by ordination, were I to pursue that route. Once, he said, "You'll probably end up more fulfilled by *your* work than I am by mine."

We faced other relational tests, too. Once, after asking about my day and listening for a while to all I had to say, Jack said, "You know, I wasn't really asking for all those *details.*"

I replied, probably more than a tad testily, "Well, you shouldn't ask me, then, because when I've asked you about your day for all these years, I've wanted to know and have listened to *all* the details!"

Of course, we experienced a lot of joy, as well as pain, through these dramatic changes. For example, I had a joyful solution to boredom during our month-long summer-camp assignments. For a few years, I was able to stay in my room guilt-free for hours on end to study because I was in graduate school. One year, we hired a sitter to accompany Jack and the kids while I stayed home taking a clinical pastoral education course. Another year, we hired a sitter so I could work on the camp staff as head women's counselor.

One of the biggest issues we faced with me going back to school, however, was finding the money for tuition and books. I did obtain a good financial aid package from ANTS and a bit of help from our local parish, but I was not able to get financial aid from the Episcopal diocese because I was not seeking ordination. Since Jack and I had always been involved in lay ministry, and since I didn't feel led to work in a church setting, I did not want to further the notion that ordination is essential for ministry. Also, for us as Episcopalians, being ordained meant becoming a priest. For most of my life, *priest* had meant *celibate male,* and I simply couldn't relate. The ordination of women in the Episcopal Church had only been regularized (officially recognized nationally) in 1976, so there were very few women priests around. Had we still been in the Congregational Church, I think I would easily have said yes to becoming ordained a *minister*. In fact, I believe that all Christians are ministers in one way or another because we are all called to serve the world.

I had put so much time and effort into my first course that Jack felt I might as well carry a full load in order to finish more quickly. I, of course, loved the idea and started doing so my second semester. I also began exploring employment options and taking all kinds of vocational tests. One career path identified by the tests really drew me—hospital chaplaincy. I had long been attracted to the worlds of science and medicine but hadn't been able to pursue them because I was so immersed in the liberal arts. Hospital chaplaincy would bring it all together for me.

The catch was that in order to get a job in hospital chaplaincy, one needed "ecclesiastical endorsement," the seal of approval by a denomination. Ordination to the priesthood was the only endorsement path the Episcopal Diocese of Massachusetts offered. Some dioceses were considering ordination to the "permanent diaconate" for such a ministry, but not mine, although I pushed for it. Friends would say to me, "If you feel called to this ministry, and ordination is required for it, then you are being called to get ordained." But that didn't sit well with me. Applying for the priesthood was too big, too deep, too personal a step. And not only for me. My daughter Amy, then around eleven or twelve, was so horrified by the thought of her mother becoming a priest that she declared she would run away from home if I pursued it.

When one is enrolled in a seminary in Boston, one is eligible to take courses in any of the eight or so other seminaries in the area. So in my second year, I took a course called Ministry Lay and Ordained at the Episcopal Divinity School (EDS) in Cambridge. There I learned that the call to priesthood was understood to be, at its core, a call to the ministries of *Word and Sacrament*. The diaconate (office of deacon), on the other hand, was specifically for those called to serve as a bridge between the church and the world, while all the other gifts of the Spirit—counseling, teaching, administration, and so forth—supported the callings of lay people. I *knew* that I felt called to biblical theology, to a ministry of the word. Gradually, through this course, the ministry of the sacrament began to seem like the outward expression of that inward call. At that point, I could honestly say I was called to ordination as a priest, so I applied. Fortunately, Amy had softened a bit by then and just asked that I never let any of her friends see me in a clerical collar. Fortunately, too, this meant the diocese would help support my education financially.

Shortly after submitting my application and all the initial paperwork, I had another huge awakening. One Saturday, we went to Cape Cod with all four kids to attend the ordination into a Pentecostal denomination of a good friend and fellow youth worker. It took place in a kind of town hall with a big stage that held a podium, a microphone, and about ten suited men seated in a row. Below the stage to one side was a woman pianist to accompany the singing. Aromas of brewing coffee and the voices of women preparing for the reception wafted up from downstairs. The service itself took well over two hours and was all about "the men of God" whom God called to lead "His" people. All the readings were about male heroes of the faith. The several talks were about these heroes, as well as about the "men of God" on the stage and the "man of God" about to be ordained.

I sat there thinking, *What am I doing? Not one person here would believe that a woman should be ordained. In fact, most of Christendom doesn't believe in it, including all those in the Roman Catholic and Orthodox traditions. I'm no activist, no prophet! I don't want this. I'm not going ahead with it!* Meanwhile, light bulbs were flashing in my head as I thought, *No wonder the world is in such a mess. Fully half of "the body of Christ" isn't free to use its gifts! Women can play the piano or cook and do helpful chores around the church, but we can't take on any real leadership, and our vision and perspectives are neither valued nor accepted.*

Anger rose up in me at this injustice, and I felt my face get red. At the same time, I felt like weeping on behalf of our world and women everywhere. These revelations were so powerful that it seemed God was calling me to stand up in the crowd and proclaim the truths I was seeing. Instead I began saying to myself, *No, that's not me. I'm not going to stand up and speak here. I will not do that!* Awareness of my absolute refusal of what seemed like a divine request rendered me somewhat dizzy, faint, and sick to my stomach. As this inner conflict went on and on, I started feeling that, like Jacob, I was wrestling with an angel. I began to wonder if the whole experience was a sign that my ministry was just going to be about empowering women, which felt somewhat insignificant and trivial. That was another sickening thought as I realized what it said about me as a woman. It was an early awakening to what I would now call my own internalized misogyny.

This inward wrestling went on for the whole length of the service. I never did stand up and speak, but I did decide to leave my application to the priesthood in place. I realize now that this experience launched me not only into the priesthood, but also into becoming a woman warrior for justice—into the desire for an archetype like Eris to encourage my continuing awakenings and subsequent work.

The ordination process in the Diocese of Massachusetts at that time had become intense and adversarial in tone, in part because the drawn-out and controversial 1976 decision by the national church to regularize the earlier, initially deemed irregular, ordinations of eleven women in Philadelphia had led to an influx of women applicants in Massachusetts, one of the few dioceses that would accept them. At that time, there were very few church positions available in the diocese for new clergy, so the many steps in the process designed to discern someone's call and qualifications were being treated more like obstacles and challenges to winnow the field. These steps included applications and autobiographical pieces to submit, one's spiritual journey and vision for ministry to describe, physical and psychological screenings to pass, the support of a local parish to secure, week-long national exams to take, and many interviews by sometimes skeptical individuals and committees to endure.

The most daunting hurdle of all was the week-long national exams. These cover such subjects as theology, church history, biblical studies, ethics, parish life, pastoral issues, and church liturgy. One must pass each subject or be reexamined in it until passing. In preparation, I joined a study group at the Episcopal Divinity School, where we succeeded mostly in making each other more anxious. Everyone had different lists of details to learn, materials to gather, and books to read, as well as countless horror stories to share. Despite my history of academic success, I felt quite insecure facing these exams, in large part because I hadn't grown up Episcopalian so didn't have church lore in my bones, as did my study mates. But, once again, I surprised myself by passing all the areas the first time around. You'd think I'd have begun to trust in my ability to do well on tests by now, but challenging new situations continued to strike me as uniquely scary. My self-confidence had a lot of growing to do.

I eventually made it through all the other obstacles and interviews in the ordination process. By June 1981, when I was finally approved and ordained a deacon, the first step toward priesthood, I wondered if I'd made it because, along with being gifted study-wise, I was just too much of a people pleaser, too used to being a *good girl.*

Seminary was also quite challenging, what with four young adolescents at home, a husband in full-time ministry, and never-ending household chores. Jack was very helpful and supportive, but home life had long been in my hands and change is hard, plus my course work was very demanding. However, it was also deeply satisfying. I kept within the required number of credits for graduation but was happily able to incorporate extra biblical studies courses in Hebrew and Greek and an extra clinical pastoral education (CPE) course to prepare for chaplaincy—one at Deaconess Hospital two days a week for a school year and one at Boston City Hospital full-time for a summer.

These CPE courses are opportunities to serve as a chaplain while studying about grief and other relevant subjects, writing up patient cases, and meeting with the staff and other seminarians to process one's encounters and experiences. The work is made intensely personal and intentionally difficult because its purpose is to prepare students for the many challenges they might encounter in their ministries. For example, at one CPE group session, a fellow was processing his grief at the death of a very young patient with whose family he had worked. He soon realized he was feeling so vulnerable because he had a young son. While he talked, tears welled up inside me, but I held them back, not knowing their cause and not wanting to fall apart in front of the group. As I fought the tears, the whole room started to spin. I could hardly believe I was carrying a grief big enough to make me faint but had no clue as to what it was. I also sensed that under the grief was guilt.

Thankfully, I had hours at home alone that night after the children were in bed. I pursued the roots of this huge grief and guilt by going back in my memories, following Agnes Sanford's recommendations in *The Healing Light*. I found myself going back to the crib death of my brother David's three-month-old baby, Jacob. My dear brother lost this son while I still had Josh, born on the same day the year before. David's marriage, right out of high school and shortly after he signed up for four years in the Marines, had been filled with challenges. He'd spent his final fourteen months of duty in Vietnam, so he'd missed that time with his firstborn son, as well as the whole first year of his daughter's life. Jacob's birth had been the beginning of healing for him and his wife, but this death was probably the beginning of the end of their marriage, although they did have several more years together and another beautiful son (whose photograph adorns the cover of this book). As I recognized my deep and lingering grief for Jacob's death, I realized that I also felt somehow guilty for it and that my guilt was rooted in a feeling of responsibility that David had married so young in the first place. I subconsciously feared he had been vulnerable because I had tormented him so as a child, envious that he was Mom's favorite. As is often the case, once one gets to the roots of a psychological complex like this, it starts to unravel. I quickly saw that David's marriage would have taken place no matter how good a big sister I had been. I understood that I could fully share in his grief for Jacob without the underlying devastation of guilt.

Reading Sanford's book that night led me to realize that there was still more to my grief than this story. Sanford suggests going back in memory to the time when you first stopped being happy. Since I couldn't remember ever feeling happiness, I kept going back until I came to the in-utero time of my mom's brother's death shortly before I was born, a story I wrote about in the first chapter. Who knows how profoundly a mother's emotions affect the baby in her womb? I'm surmising, and we are learning now, that they affect it quite a lot. That night, I also came to new understandings of Mom's grief, especially in light of her early father issues and his clear preference for her younger sister and brother. Perhaps, for example, she had been jealous of Chester and, ruing her feelings after his death, couldn't bear to see my jealous, competitive behavior with David.

These realizations released in me great compassion for Mom and opened the way for more healing in our relationship. It also made a difference in how I was mothering my own children. I began to see that much of their behavior was normal sibling rivalry rather than something I had to curtail. I became determined that the generational patterns of critical parenting I had inherited would stop with me—that I would do the healing work necessary so as not to pass these patterns on to my children. I remain deeply grateful to Agnes Sanford for these insights and also for teaching me that we all naturally desire and pray for the healing of a sick child or loved one. We long to know that our touch, presence, and loving intentions make a difference. I strongly believe that healing prayer—of whatever sort, wordless or otherwise—is an aspect of what we are all called to offer one another.

During my time in seminary, I also faced anew my dread of being put on a pedestal because it emerged full force whenever a professor complimented me publicly about my work. As I probed the depths of this fear more fully, I saw that it was rooted in my mom's response to the way her parents doted on me. I came to the realization that she had always been trying to *knock me off the pedestal* her parents had put me on: No wonder I had come to believe subconsciously that *pedestals are dangerous places*! Many years later, shortly before her death from cancer in 1988, my mom actually confirmed that this had been her intention. During one of my visits with her that year I asked, "Mom, when I was little, did you feel you needed to knock me off the pedestal my grandparents put me on?" Her most enlightening and lovingly intended response was, "Oh, yes. They would have spoiled you so!" By that point, our relationship on all fronts had greatly healed, so these words from her were merely the frosting on the cake. But frosting, and confirmation, are so good— and often so needed. Furthermore, she had done this lovingly— for my own good—because in her mind, a *spoiled* little girl could become an independent and selfish little girl, a girl who wanted her own way. How, then, could she be happy in her predestined role as a wife and mother?

This *pedestal dread* was really put to the test during my last semester at ANTS. I was chosen by the faculty to give the student graduation address because, despite my four adolescent children and demanding home life, I was first in my class and the recipient of a couple of biblical studies awards. Several friends told me that this was absolutely *not* the kind of request one turns down, although I desperately wanted to do so. In the end, preparing for and delivering that speech was a powerful learning experience for me and established a lifelong conviction about its theme: *I want to see. I want to see what I and the institutions of which I am a part are saying by our actions.* It seems that nowadays many, many people are being convinced of this need to *see* what's really going on with our institutions and government. There is increasing awareness that we need to wake up and take action—on one level or another and for one cause or another—for the sake of all people and life on our planet.

My talk at graduation was based on the John 9 story of Jesus healing the man born blind. The man is challenged about his version of the healing over and over by the religious authorities of the day. Each time he has to respond, his clarity about the event and his insight into Jesus deepens. He *sees*! It took courage for me to give what was an honest and personal speech with political overtones because at the time there were some serious issues going on at ANTS. I had been processing it all because, serendipitously, I was just finishing a course at EDS on systems analysis, specifically looking at an institution's *espoused theory* versus its *theory in action*. So when I was asked to give the speech, although my first thought had been, *I don't have anything to say*, my second thought was, *I have too much to say! How will I say it, and dare I try?* In the end, I did try. In my speech, I proclaimed: "I want to see!" And now, many years later, I seek in this book, in effect, to *channel* Eris, the archetype who isn't afraid to challenge the established authorities and who, in the process, illuminates what our actions and the actions of our institutions reveal about who we really are and what we really believe.

During this emotionally stressful period of completing school, searching for a job, and preparing the commencement address, I experienced a strong bodily reaction. The early symptoms were red and painful eyes, blurred vision, and an intense sensitivity to light. I was diagnosed with iritis, a symptomatic inflammatory condition in the iris, which is a complication from any number of possible diseases. The treatment is cortisone drops, which alleviate the symptoms but are not a safe long-term solution. So here I was giving a speech on the subject *I want to see*, and my eyes were inflamed and my vision blurry. I couldn't help but ask myself, *What am I not want-ing to see? Or is there something I am seeing that is inflaming me?*

Because this iritis recurred every few months, particularly in times of stress, my doctor tried a range of tests to identify its root cause. But it wasn't until four or five years later that an explor-atory chest X-ray finally revealed some enlarged nodes in my lungs that indicated sarcoidosis, an autoimmune, multisystemic disease of unknown origin that sometimes causes iritis—a diagnosis that was confirmed by surgery. Though sarcoidosis can become chronic, even occasionally fatal, it usually becomes asymptomatic in time, which—apart from a few minor skin eruptions—thankfully became true in my case.

When first diagnosed, however, I was informed that in the early 1900s, sarcoidosis primarily affected indigent Black males and was often fatal. Later in the century, it seemed primarily to affect mid-dle-class white women and was fairly benign. *Mmm*, I wondered, *what is it that we two groups of people have in common? What do I need to see or learn here? If in autoimmune diseases the body is attack-ing, not recognizing, itself, how is that subconsciously true for me? In Black men, might it have been an expression of internalized racism, and in me, an expression of internalized misogyny?*

While I can't say that I came to any further clarity about all this, I can say that living with sarcoidosis has led to much inner reflec-tion and an ever-deepening awareness of the importance of listen-ing to my body and trusting its wisdom. Anyone with the diagno-sis of a chronic condition likely experiences this kind of awakening, but it is such an important lesson for us all to learn. Our lives tend to involve way too much negativity and unhealthy stress—plus our very times are incredibly stressful. Greater awareness of and atten-tion to our bodies' needs, as well as to the needs of our communities, are essential to health and well-being. Fortunately, resources abound, but alas, so does misinformation. Transformation is needed at all levels if we are to bring about greater health for ourselves, our com-munities, and our planet.

Shortly after giving the commencement address and receiving the iritis diagnosis, I was ordained to the diaconate with four other peo-ple at the Cathedral Church of St. Paul in Boston. A year later, on

June 9, 1982, St. Columba's Day, I was ordained a priest at our home church, Parish of the Messiah in Newton. Both were awesome, humbling, and moving events. For the second, I asked my Hebrew studies teacher and good friend Dr. Carole Fontaine, the John Taylor professor of biblical theology and history at Andover Newton, to preach. She was stellar! She talked about St. Columba, who was credited with bringing Christianity from Ireland to the British Isles by way of an abbey he founded on the Scottish Island of Iona. I had chosen this date in large part because Jack and I had once visited Iona with my parents and found it to be a magical place, so much so that we have since visited it again twice. In her charge to me, Carole said, "Go found your own Iona." This proved to be quite a prophetic charge because ten years later I moved to Maine to help found Greenfire, a spiritual retreat center for women.

I remember two early but particularly powerful experiences of serving as a woman priest. The first one was at a women's Cursillo, a spiritual renewal weekend. The liturgical leaders there were all male Episcopal priests. However, one learned that I was ordained and privately, graciously, said to me, "I'm scheduled to celebrate at the final communion service, but I think it's only right that you should do it in my place." The other women did not know I was ordained because personal sharing hadn't been encouraged, so it was a moving moment when I stepped up from among them in this emotional, spiritually charged environment and offered the communion service on behalf of us all. I felt anointed as I did so, as if some balance of power in the room was shifting and we women were all sensing our legitimate place at the altar. Several shed a few tears and expressed much gratitude for this new and enlightening experience.

The second took place at a Young Life conference for staff women (thankfully, we were no longer referred to as staff *girls*). Many powerful women presenters led sessions, Jack and I sat on a panel about staff marriage relationships, and a few of us put together a final worship service. I was to preach and to lead communion while other clergywomen led other parts. I prepared a sermon on the Luke 13:10–17 story of the bent-over woman whom Jesus healed on the Sabbath and who, in response, led the people in praise and worship. However, as the time for the service approached, the president of Young Life, known and beloved for his humorous and powerful speaking abilities, called me aside and said to me, "Judy, I just want you to know that I will be the preacher today. I'm all prepared, and I think that would be expected."

He seemed to assume that I would be grateful and simply acquiesce. I was quite taken aback but quickly found myself responding with absolute conviction, "No, you can't. This is a women's conference, and we are meant to lead it. I'm all prepared, too. Besides, my sermon is specifically about the valid place of women in leading worship, so I need to preach it!" In short order, he was the one who acquiesced.

That day and over the years since, I have heard from many women what a powerful and pivotal experience the whole service was for them. Many came from conservative churches where ordaining women was not even being contemplated. That service allowed them to feel what they were missing and to discover they were actually craving confirmation of their own equality with men, their own holiness.

In contrast to these experiences of blessing within a circle of women, every one of us who became a priest in those early years also experienced the opposite—discomfort, displeasure, even disdain— from several of the male Episcopal priests with whom we came in contact. This was particularly noticeable to me at clergy conferences, where some men would walk by and not only not acknowledge my presence, but actually look dismissively up and away from me. I could almost have felt sorry for them had it not been so painful.

My theory was that for many of these men the legitimacy of women priests threatened the specialness of their own role. One man had articulated something like that to me during a private interview early on in the ordination process. He had asked, "Tell me, why do you want to be a priest anyway? It just means you get to say certain words on certain occasions. Why go through all this for that?"

I had stammered my usual response about my sense of being called to the ministry of word and sacrament, of service to the presence of the Holy in our midst. But the dispirited tone of this priest's voice and the way he asked his question said to me that he was in doubt about his own worth as well as that of the priestly ministry. I sensed he feared that women being allowed to do the same things he did would further demean both him and his work because it would take away not only his sense of privilege, but also much of the mystery of his power.

I must say that thirty-plus years ago I had far warmer receptions from several Roman Catholic priests than from some male priests in my own denomination. Thankfully, the times they've been a-changin' on many fronts, as well as, sadly, regressing these days on many others.

Chapter 8

Serving Diversity

In the spring of 1981, besides finishing seminary course work and preparing for ordination—plus, in my case, writing a commencement address—my classmates and I were all seeking jobs. I had heard that Deaconess Hospital in Boston, where I had worked during one of my clinical pastoral education courses, was expecting to add a full-time chaplain position. I applied and prayed I would get it since this is an excellent hospital and since, as far as I knew, there were no other such positions available in the greater Boston area. However, about the time the head of the chaplaincy department at Deaconess called and offered me the position, I also received a call from the head of Groton School, an Episcopal college-preparatory school in Groton, Massachusetts. He said that I had been recommended as a candidate for their school chaplain position by John Coburn, my bishop, who knew Jack and me and our years of work with young people quite well.

I was ignorant about the private school world so had never considered that kind of chaplaincy work. But I realized that working at a school, unlike at a hospital, would leave me free to be with my family during summers and school vacations. I also learned that faculty members received huge discounts on tuition, so most enrolled their children in the school. What an opportunity this might be! I immediately went for an interview and came away excited about the prospect. I also came away knowing that, if hired, I would be replacing a single woman who lived in single-person housing, whereas I would be bringing a family of six, including four children eligible to receive the tuition discount. The bishop hadn't mentioned this small fact to the school when he recommended me. The folks who conducted the interview were all very cordial and welcoming, but, not surprisingly, they soon offered the position to a single woman.

All of a sudden I was in a quandary. I no longer wanted my dream job at Deaconess. Instead I wanted a job I didn't get. *What was this upheaval all about?* I wondered. *What should I do now?* Fortunately, I was able to delay my response to Deaconess for a couple of weeks, during which time I got another call, again thanks to Bishop Coburn.

Dana Hall School for Girls, a non-religiously affiliated international day and boarding school located in Wellesley, Massachusetts, near where we lived, was seeking a chaplain to replace an interim who was an Episcopal priest. That man had asked the bishop for any recommendations and was urged to consider me. This was a very different prospect from Groton because we would not have to move and because only our daughters might qualify for tuition discounts, although in the end neither chose to attend Dana. I applied immediately and soon began a long process of tours and interviews with everyone from a few students and teachers to the counselor, the dean of students and other administrators, the head of the school, and one or two trustees. I liked the place and the people a lot and certainly wanted the job. However, the search committee was not planning to make a decision immediately, and the deadline for deciding about the chaplaincy position at Deaconess Hospital was looming. I explained my dilemma to the key people at Dana and waited, on pins and needles, as they say, for a week or so until finally, thankfully, I was offered the position.

I worked at Dana Hall from the fall of 1981 through the end of the 1993 school year, twelve amazing, challenging, difficult, and wonderful years. The intuition I had had that my ministry might prove to be about women was verified because I was immersed for those twelve years in learning about the educational and life issues of young women from all over the world. My chaplaincy role of spiritual presence and guide for the whole school community was relatively undefined since Dana Hall was a secular school with no chapel or religious services, but there were certainly high hopes and expectations. Fortunately, the whole community was kind and forgiving for the most part as I fumbled my way along.

One of the earliest questions I faced was, "What would you like us to tell the students they should call you—Reverend, Pastor, Mrs. Carpenter?" (Thankfully, no one suggested *Mother*, which was what the priest at our home parish wanted since he was definitely *Father*!)

I knew that I didn't want to go by any of these titles, but I wasn't sure what would be appropriate. In my work with young people up to that point, I had always gone by the first name I'd grown up with, Judy. However, I'd never liked the name because, when linked with my maiden name—Judy Perry—it felt like a double diminutive. So I queried, "What are the other adults called?"

"Oh, everyone uses Mr., Mrs., Ms., or Dr. with their last name," I was told.

"Isn't there anyone who uses their first name?" I asked.

The answer was, "Let's see...ahh, Rosanna, the counselor does."

Now, Rosanna had been part of the team who hired me, and we were already becoming friends. So without a lot of thought, out of my mouth popped the words, "Well then, they can call me Judith." And I've been Judith, happily and officially, ever since.

At the time, it was important to me not to distance myself or my role as a clergyperson from the girls, so I wanted to go by my first name, not a title. I imagined how liberating it would be for them to grow up thinking of women clergy as a natural, familiar phenomenon. Also, despite Amy's squeamishness about seeing me in a clerical collar, I decided to wear one at the school a couple of days a week to normalize it. My deepest spirituality had always been about inclusiveness—*everyone is welcome*—and I wanted my chaplaincy in this diverse international community to represent that. I don't remember anyone explicitly asking me about the collar, but I know I intentionally articulated my reasons for wearing it on a few occasions. In any case, despite my role or dress, I found that I was quickly able to establish the easy, friendly rapport with most of the girls that I had experienced with young people in the past.

During my time at Dana, I was privileged to work with some amazing and gifted people, both students and adults. Many of the latter became close friends. In 1986, Jack and I happily agreed to move into campus housing, again with the encouragement of the bishop, who thought school chaplaincy was the perfect place for me. (He actually said, "Most priests can serve in parishes, but very few can do the bridge-building work in the world that you are able to do.") The move allowed us to rent our Newton house, which helped finance our children's college educations. It also brought us much more intimately into campus life and allowed Jack to become fully a part of the school community. He loved eating most of his meals in the dining center, befriending the girls, and hobnobbing with the staff at all levels. He was in his element because he had no responsibilities but could be his best supportive, listening, caring self. And, of course, he was much loved and trusted in return.

So, here I was, chaplain of an international secular school with no chapel and with girls from all the major religious traditions, as well as many with no religious affiliation. As one of two in-house counselors, my job primarily involved being available to whomever wanted to talk or needed help. I was also there to make sure the girls felt supported in their own religious traditions or lack thereof. Needless to say, my ignorance on many fronts was deep and my learning curve steep.

It was also my job to offer prayers—either an invocation and benediction or some other prayer of blessing—for all significant school events and gatherings. *How, I wondered, can I presume to pray in such a way that everyone will feel included, even those who are turned off by the word God? What words can I use to ensure that the students, who are teenagers, after all, won't sit there rolling their eyes?* I struggled so to find language that would be honest and from my heart as well as convey or invite some opening to Mystery—to love, spirit, the source, the life force—on the part of the students, staff, parents, trustees, or guests present. This deep and ongoing work of seeking to find words that might address, hold, support, and even encourage the spirituality of the diverse individuals within all levels of the school community pushed me way beyond the confines of my own tradition and out into a territory with few models—a territory that eventually came to feel like home base to me.

In time, along with some teaching and administrative responsibilities, I became the advisor of three significant student groups on campus: my own Chaplain's Advisory Board, composed of students from each of the religious traditions represented on campus; the Grief Group, composed of students who had suffered major loss and wanted a safe place to process that; and the support group for Black and Hispanic students, which named itself Women of Color (WOC). Each of these groups graced me with incredibly rich relationships with a wide range of students and opened my eyes to many of the issues they faced.

One particularly meaningful program the Chaplain's Advisory Board offered was a discussion group on diverse topics that was open to the whole school and held biweekly over supper in a small side dining room. The discussion that most stands out in my mind happened in mid-January 1991 during Desert Storm. The United States had commenced extensive aerial bombing of Iraq to end the occupation of Kuwait, and Iraq retaliated with a Scud missile attack on Israel that the U.S. tried to intercept over Saudi Arabia. We had students at Dana Hall from Iraq, Iran, Saudi Arabia, Israel, and Palestine. These girls were classmates together, but suddenly some of their countries, at the instigation of the U.S., were bombing each other. They came into the small dining room that night full of questions: "Can anybody reach parents or family members?" "Does anyone know what's happening now?" "Are any other countries getting involved yet?" Mostly, though, they were each just overwhelmed with emotions—from terror to grief to rage. "I can't believe this is happening! How did it start?" "I'm just so afraid for my family—I keep imaging our home being bombed!" "Will it ever be safe to live in my country again?" There were slight overtones of strain between those whose countries had a history of hostilities, but the dominant tone was camaraderie and mutual compassion. They seemed so relieved to be with classmates who understood their anxiety—and temporarily away from those who were less personally affected by this raw experience of the terror of war.

As for the Grief Group, these girls came together to help one another feel less alone and more able to deal with whatever tragedy had befallen them, be it illness, accident, divorce, death, suicide, whatever—we had it all. Some stayed with the group for years while others moved on after a time. Often, someone would bring a student she thought could use the group and help her become part of it. We all gradually experienced the truth that deep loss, pain, and grief do not go away, but rather, in time and with loving support, people can discover more space inside themselves for life to continue and for new joys, new possibilities, to emerge. This is the path by which any one of us becomes a *wounded healer*. After learning the hard way to hold the paradoxical pain of suffering and the joy of life together within ourselves, we can more fully be with others in both.

The group with which I had the most extensive involvement was the sizable Women of Color club, which was in charge, among other things, of the all-school Rev. Dr. Martin Luther King Jr. Convocation. This was one powerful collection of young women! They had to be, going to school in this privileged setting in predominantly white Wellesley. Knowing I had a mixed-race family probably helped them welcome me into their midst—plus they all thought John David was pretty cute—so I got to hear about the subtle and not-so-subtle discrimination they experienced on an almost daily basis in the school and the town. They would talk about being followed in stores by personnel clearly suspicious that they were there to steal something, or of walking down the sidewalk and having people cross the street to avoid coming near them. Their stories of personal pain, struggle, and courage further challenged and awakened me to issues not only of race, but also of class.

One year, these WOC girls worked together to create a display case in the main hall of the classroom building on the subject "What Sustains Me." We draped the shelves of the case with a lovely purple satin cloth. Then they each added personal objects, pictures, clothing, ethnic art, books, poems—anything that symbolized inner strength and sustenance to them as they sought to survive, and indeed thrive, in the world of Dana Hall. When we gathered to talk about the whole experience after the display was completed, the president of the club listened a bit and then turned to me and said, "You should interview us about all this and write it up so we can each keep a copy." I happily did so and put together an article honoring them, which they all read and approved. It was titled "Voices: Women of Color" and was published in the fall 1991 issue of *Independent School* magazine.

When we gathered for these interviews, I launched us off by saying, "Let's begin by talking about the way the club serves and supports you in your life here."

Pretty quickly, their answers flowed. One said, "We can relax together because we don't have to feel like anyone is watching us or censoring us. Mostly, we can just say whatever we want to say...pretty freely."

Another commented, "You know, for me the best thing about the club is that it's a place to just laugh things off...because, think about it, what else can you do?"

The club president then cautioned, "Judith, don't make it sound like we don't appreciate being here at Dana, though. It's helping us learn to live and deal with all kinds of people, right?" Affirmative nods all around.

One girl added, "After all, you can't expect anyplace to be perfect." A few laughs.

A quiet but thoughtful girl mused, "We know we have to be strong, so it's hard to say, 'Something is wrong.' Instead, we keep saying, 'I have to work this out on my own.' Really we're all a little taken aback and frightened here." Again, nods all around.

"Basically," another said, "we'd rather be home. People don't understand that we give up a lot to be here. But we can tolerate this environment for what the education can give us: options for the future...status...so we can make a difference and have people listen to us someday. After all, we're just here for a while."

A few talked about the shock of coming to Dana Hall for the first time. One said, "I come from a predominantly Black neighborhood where you hardly ever see a white person, so I just always believed I was equal."

Another noted, "There are so many differences that people don't recognize, even teachers. But you just can't argue with some of those teachers, and sometimes they make assumptions about a society that are just plain *wrong*—you're *from* there and you know."

"Actually," the previous speaker said, "we can't really talk to anybody—at school or at home. It's like we don't really belong here, but we don't really belong at home anymore either. People there say, 'You've changed.' But there's nothing we can do about that."

One girl added, "People at home try to be encouraging about what this education will mean for my future. But I'm a person and I have feelings, which are not just about education. I'm in the middle of the transformation from being a girl to becoming a woman, and I can't really talk about it to anybody."

This comment led another to say, "I'm tired of having to be so strong and always having my guard up. The reason Black women are strong is because they've had to be to survive, but if I could really depend on someone, I'd do it in a minute."

These students were struggling against great odds to claim their dignity and believe in their choices—in their power to make changes for the better for themselves and ultimately for their communities. Their insights and questions pose great challenges to schools and to all of us who are not people of color because these are things we simply cannot see. Without an analysis of the power structures that keep the systems of oppression in place, and without an alternative vision of justice and right relations, we not only participate in injustice, but we perpetuate the tendency to "blame the victim."

During my years at Dana Hall, many schools were beginning to address white privilege, internalized racism, and discrimination of all sorts. Part of my job became helping to bring in or create diversity workshops for both students and faculty. Soon we also began dealing with homophobia and started a group on campus, modeled after those emerging at many private schools, for girls to talk about lesbian, gay, transgender, and straight issues. This was no small thing because many of our students came from traditional families that were not supportive of the school starting such a group. We prevailed because we knew the risk of self-harm or suicide for young people who felt that they were or might be homosexual or that their assigned gender didn't fit their self-understanding. Not only did they desperately need support, but the rest of us needed to understand and have compassionate respect for their reality. All of this diversity work helped wake me up to the interconnected and systemic structures of oppression that permeate life in this country, structures that those in privileged positions—which is to say white, male, heterosexual, healthy, able-bodied, middle- or upper-class people—don't have to and usually don't want to see.

As we all know at some level, for real inner change to happen, one must allow oneself to be stretched and broken open by new experiences and encounters. We can be guaranteed that such encounters will indeed come. Our choice is whether to receive and learn from them or to resist and fight them. Moving from simplistic black/white, either/or thinking to both/and thinking, to a genuine openness and receptivity of difference, and maybe even to a delight in mystery and paradox, is a long and frightening journey. Although I had always been drawn to the big picture, always delighted when my internal boxes were broken open, always believed in greater inclusion, I was unexpectedly taken much further along on this journey by virtue of my job at Dana Hall. Many of my narrower Christian beliefs began to crumble during that time as I experienced the beauty of other faiths through the young women I came to know and love. So, too, did my unconscious homophobia as I heard the questions and sexual-identity struggles of several of them. It would be many years before same-sex couples would be allowed to marry in this country, but my eventual delight in participating in and celebrating such unions began way back there at Dana Hall.

As I think of all that was going on while I was a chaplain, I think also of my parallel awakening to the gender bias of the English language for humans and, especially troublesome, our language about God. This was bound to happen in the context of an all-girls school where I had to offer public prayers, but it took attendance at the 1984 Evangelical and Ecumenical Women's Conference in Wellesley for me—and for Jack, who also attended—to grapple in depth with male language for the God dimension. In retrospect, I am struck by my resistance to realizing that, for forty or more years, I had not let this bother me much. I think that was because, like many women, I was reluctant to face the fact that, at some level, gender-biased language marginalized me, and that a God, Christ, and Holy Spirit as Father, Lord, King, He, and Him stays "Other" for women. Such language as goddess, Sophia, Mother, Jesus as brother, the Holy as She, on the other hand, touches some deep place inside once it is welcomed and understood as equally true of the great mystery to which all such language refers.

Furthermore, for me, Mary the mother of Jesus as gentle receptive vessel was not a large enough container for womanhood. I longed for the whole range of feminine saints, warriors, common folk, even witches and goddesses, to free up and grow into the fullness of myself. Something awoke in me as I recognized this, recalled my old love of fairy-tale heroines and goddess archetypes, and began learning and experimenting on my own. I discovered a real hunger and began to fill it with research into the roots of language, symbols, and forms of worship. I vividly remember my excitement on first reading *The Chalice and the Blade: Our History, Our Future*, by Riane Eisler, because it opened up the possibility, however controversial, that human society has not always been patriarchally structured. Therefore, other models are possible. When the new dwarf planet Eris was discovered, my awakening to the transformative potential of her archetype was particularly moving—indeed, it inspired me to write this book with its invitation to an enhanced awareness of oneness and a greater consciousness of the imperative of global inclusion in the party of life.

One dramatic expression of the power of honoring the full feminine came with the 1989 consecration of Barbara Harris as the first woman bishop in the worldwide Anglican Communion, which took place at Hynes Auditorium in Boston before a congregation of nearly 8,000 people. As a diocesan priest, I had the great privilege of campaigning and voting for her election and then processing as part of the official entourage at the service. That small-of-stature but powerfully dynamic African-American woman, in gorgeous multicolored robes that hid the bulletproof vest she had been urged to wear, took the stage for all women that day. What a courageous and prophetic witness she was then and throughout her ministry as she held her own in countless bastions of male power. To me, she is a model of the archetypal woman warrior of the Spirit that I see in the Eris archetype and to which I believe we all, men and women alike, are called in these toxic times.

Chapter 9

Dreaming Greenfire

While all this growth, challenge, and change was going on in the context of my work life at Dana Hall, our children were becoming teenagers, and our home life was becoming increasingly dysfunctional. John David and Amy, although over a year apart in age, were in the same grade since John David had had a slower start in school, and Josh was just one year behind them. Therefore, they all knew the same kids, so opportunities for trouble to spread were manifold. For example, any gathering one of them might have when we weren't there could easily turn into a major party. Although, like most parents, it took years for us to learn all that went on behind our backs or when we were away, we discovered a great deal at the time because someone would slip, confess, worry, ask for help, or something.

John David was becoming increasingly silent, sullen, belligerent, and just plain angry as he grew older. I can still hear his sneered, "You can't make me!" His rage seemed to focus on me, the primary disciplinarian, and his scornful glares would turn me cold. Also, from the beginning he had targeted Amy, the former oldest child, so we tried to be vigilant about protecting her from any abuse. And we feared that he often bullied Josh in their large shared attic bedroom, although Josh never complained. We eventually fixed up the small guest bedroom for Josh so he could have his own safe space. That left John David with the whole attic, and we soon discovered that he was gouging knife holes all over the walls. When we confronted him about this, he had no explanation and just shrugged it off as no big deal. Meanwhile, Jack and I couldn't seem to agree on how to deal with any of this. He believed part of the problem was that I overreacted and was way too strict, especially with John David. I was convinced that he *under*reacted and didn't take things seriously enough. We did acknowledge to one another, though, that we were both becoming afraid that our oldest son might explode in some unforeseen and possibly dangerous way.

The other kids had clearly become somewhat afraid of John David, too, because they were very careful not to cross him and avoided him as much as possible. Amy, who always tried to be a very caring and helpful person despite John David's attitude toward her, would let on that she was worried about him but could give no specifics. She was also in the middle of her own teenage-girl emotional storms so added many dramatic scenes to the household. She felt particularly unheard by me and, in exasperated tears, would say things like, "I just can't talk to you about anything, Mom. You'll never, ever understand me!" (Often, paradoxically, the very next day, some Dana student would break down in tears in my office and tell me all about her own mother's failures—which would sound very familiar—and end up saying, "I'm so glad I can talk to you because you really understand me.")

As for Josh, he just seemed to tune us all out as much as possible—a worrisome sign. And Anna reacted to everything in her own feisty or fearful way. She would beg us not to fight with John David, the adopted big brother with whom she closely identified, saying, "Stop fighting. Just stop it! I'm afraid he's going to run away!"

All in all, Jack and I were quite overwhelmed and badly in need of help, but, like many parents, somewhat in denial of our own fearful intuitions about that need. Also like many, we did not know where to turn or whom to trust with such deeply personal stuff.

Eventually, blessedly, a friend recommended a family systems counselor, whom I'll call Fran, and Jack and I finally went to her in desperation. After we described our family situation and issues, Fran's memorable first question was, "Who did you think you were?" She then asked "Why didn't you bring the kids in with you? I'll need to talk with them and get their perspectives, too."

In our utter helplessness, we asked, "How will we do that? They won't want to come."

Fran answered us very clearly. "Just tell them that you are going to a counselor to help you be better parents, but that the counselor needs to hear from them, too, so that she can really understand the issues. Therefore, they all need to come with you next week."

As expected, when we told the kids this, they responded, "No way!" But on the appointed day, they all got into our Volkswagen van and came with us, bickering the whole time.

Once we arrived and were all seated in a circle, Fran introduced herself to them and said, "Your parents have come to me because of some of the issues going on at home. They want help being better parents. Now, I'm not *your* counselor, but it would really help me help them if I could hear your thoughts about it all."

Her words were met with a long, awkward silence. Finally, it was Josh who spoke. "I think John David gets mad a lot and argues with my folks. Also, he and Amy get in fights sometimes, and Anna gets upset about that and about a lot of things. Plus, my parents have to yell a lot because we don't always do what we're told to do." His memorable conclusion, true to his peacemaker self, was, "Personally, though, I don't really have a problem with anybody."

And so it began. On the way home that day, as we went for the promised ice cream treats, the kids were actually laughing and singing!

We worked with Fran for quite a while, sometimes with the children and sometimes alone. The first level of group conversations revealed me as the primary disciplinarian and problem parent. One of the hardest things I have ever done was to sit there quietly for several sessions, desperately trying to hold my center and trust the process, as one or the other of the kids described all my dysfunctional, hopeless tactics. For example, poor John David had spent countless hours in his room because I hadn't known what to do with him when he disobeyed badly other than say, "Go to your room!" And I washed Anna's mouth out with soap so many times that, to this day, she can't abide the smell of Ivory soap. Although the youngest, Anna was determined to compete at the level of the others. Since bad language from this feisty little one always stopped everyone in their tracks, she took to using swear words she had overheard any time she felt vulnerable, often with no idea what they meant. For example, once when calling someone "faggot" failed to get a satisfactory response, she yelled out, "You bundle of sticks!" because that was the definition for the word John David had given her.

After about five counseling sessions focused on my dictatorial but ineffective parenting, Fran asked the kids, "What about your dad?" All eyes turned to Jack as it seemed to dawn on them that he was their parent, too, although he had left most of the disciplining to me. Initially, this had been a conscious choice because Jack was committed to overcoming John David's distance and anger with love, connection, and fun, the tactic that served so well in his Young Life work with kids. He was bound and determined that this hurting boy would not make him change his style or get visibly angry. That left me holding the disciplinary bag, so to speak, especially when things got tough with John David.

Fran proved to be a miracle worker for our family. When she had Jack and me alone, she explained to us her theory. "As far as I can tell, your three younger children, who have been with you their whole lives, are fine with your parenting style. But John David is another story. I would postulate that he spent his formative years in a foster family where the father was the tough one and the mother was more soft-spoken. Therefore, he's stuck at this critical stage of his maturation process and needs you two to replicate that model. Jack, you've got to get tough—no fooling around or joking about things with him, no buddying up or letting him call you by your first name. Instead, you'll have to be the disciplinarian on every issue. And Judith, you'll have to back down, be quiet, and allow Jack to take over this responsibility."

The ensuing scenes were, in hindsight, quite a skit as John David would start something, and I would be biting my lip and glaring at Jack, silently imploring, *Hurry up and do something!* He, meanwhile, would be glaring back at me, saying, in effect, *I'll deal with it! Give me a chance!* The miracle was that Fran had *nailed* it. Very quickly, we realized that our bumbling efforts to follow her advice were working. Things stopped escalating and the whole family began to relax.

We experienced additional crises over the next few years that brought us back to Fran time and again, but she was equal to our needs. For example, on one winter visit when the kids and we were complaining about all the fighting that went on around the woodstove in the living room, she asked, "Why don't you kids just go up to your rooms and get away from each other?"

Almost in unison, they answered, "Are you kidding? It's freezing up there!"

Fran looked questioningly at us, and we sheepishly explained, "Well, we've been keeping the heat down upstairs to save money."

She responded wryly, "Why don't you just turn the heat up and instead save money by not having to come see me!"

Another time, she said to Jack and me, "You know, you two are fully capable of sorting out all the issues I'm helping you address. You do this all the time for other people. Instead of paying me, why don't you use the money to go out to dinner once a week and figure things out for yourselves."

While we did turn the heat up, we never seemed able to schedule those dinners together. Managing life with two working parents and four challenging children was just too demanding. That was in the 1980s. How much worse must time pressures be on families these days?

It became clear in hindsight that John David was suffering from what has now been labeled Reactive Attachment Disorder. It's a syndrome common to adopted children, especially those who were moved from one foster family to another. All that early loss and grief leave these children unable to attach and trust. John David recently told us that it wasn't until his thirties that he understood that he really belonged to a family. Now he is totally committed to attending all significant family gatherings, like weddings and reunions—in fact, sometimes he is a prime mover in setting up these events and encouraging people to come. He has settled into stable and satisfying work in Richmond, Virginia, has bought a little house that he works at remodeling, and has made many friends—all while caring for and being involved in the lives of the many virtually fatherless kids in his neighborhood. He is a truly gentle and beautiful man—who also loves to work out and participate in extreme sports challenges like the Tough Mudder.

Our other three adult children live near us in midcoast Maine, and each in his or her own way has taken all that they've been through and used it to become beautiful healers themselves. Amy is the mother of one lovely daughter and a clinical social worker who works with kids, couples, and families. She also teaches kundalini yoga and is in the process of writing three books. Josh oversees and teaches a middle school alternative education program and is the single father of two amazing and wonderful daughters. Anna does not have the disorder that John David surely has, but she has had significant issues of her own, ranging over the years from diagnoses of attention deficit hyperactive disorder (ADHD) to anxiety and depression. In retrospect, her healing really began when she confessed to us, with the aid of the substance-abuse counselor at Dana Hall who agreed to meet with her, that she was cross-addicted to drugs and alcohol and needed help. It took stints in two rehab facilities, but Anna has now been sober since age twenty. That's approaching thirty years of sobriety in this culture of indulgence and partying! Although she has had a rough journey with many other ups and downs, Anna is now living into her most gifted and caring self, serving others through Alcoholics Anonymous, the practice of Reiki, and other healing modalities. She has two beautiful daughters. Miracles abound, indeed!

Any family that has tried to deal with serious dysfunction faces a steep learning curve personally and interpersonally. Professional help of some sort is probably always needed because no one is totally free of denial and/or selective blindness. We all need some objective, trusted eyes to mirror our issues back to us and offer sound advice. When these issues include drug and alcohol addiction, like ours did, the whole family is taken on an up-and-down journey. Everyone is called to awaken to their own addictive patterns as well as to how addiction affects family systems. And everyone is called to keep on learning because these lessons are never finished. Transformation and liberation are long, slow processes—but worth everything in the end.

Humility is another huge piece of the puzzle when it comes to healing problematic patterns. For me, remembering and recounting these stories of my side of our parenting difficulties stirred anew some deep regrets—for the many times I was in over my head but did not seek help, for the many times I followed poor, simplistic advice in sheer desperation, and for the many times I reacted to situations from my most knee-jerk, immature self. Despite all this, I remember that, when Fran asked us at one point if we had done the best parenting job we could do, I thought a while but had to reply, "Yes, I guess

I always did the very best I could—*in the moment* and *at the time.*"
I also remember a conversation with Amy some years later when
John David stumbled into serious trouble that looked irredeemable
(although it ended up being his last such incident). I was lamenting
to her what they all had gone through because of his adoption, since
it now looked like he wouldn't make it. She replied, in no uncertain terms, "Mom, enough of your guilt! Don't wish away my family—don't take away my story!" One level of my habitual self-incrim-
ination fell away with that blessed charge from my firstborn child.
Perhaps the greatest gratitude of my life at this point is that we all
have had the grace to process, individually and together, much of
our history. Although such deep work is never finished, it is the real
source of healing—and always a miracle.

Early on in the Dana Hall years, in the midst of all these family and
personal developments, I became part of a most significant and
meaningful relationship with two other chaplains, Connie Chandler-
Ward of Wellesley College and Rosaria Salerno of Boston College.
We met as often as we could, weekly when possible and even some
whole weekends, processing our work as chaplains and challenging
each other regarding the issues of our lives and of the times. We
even began dreaming and envisioning work we could do together in
the future. All that ended when Rosaria followed her political pas-
sions and, in 1987, got elected to the Boston City Council on her first
attempt at running for office—a major coup for a college chaplain
and former nun! After that, her time was no longer her own—and
certainly not Connie's and mine. However, through this relationship,
Connie and I had laid the groundwork for another threesome with
an even clearer vision to develop that same year.

This next group involved three Episcopal priests—Connie,
myself, and Rosanna Kazanjian, who had been the school counselor
at Dana Hall when I first came but who had since been ordained
and was serving in a parish. We quickly clicked as a dynamic three-
some and gradually realized that we shared a longing to do more
in-depth spiritual work with women, perhaps in some kind of retreat
center context one day. We met and dreamed together for several
years, during which time Connie and Rosanna, both widowed, fell
in love and became partners. Fortunately our shared vision and

commitment proved strong enough to hold us together as a three-some despite this intimate new twosome in our midst. It helped a lot that we were all learning to work with the Enneagram, which is a great tool for understanding and exploring differences of motivation and approach. This tool enabled the three of us to enhance our understanding and strengthen our bonds throughout this time of changing relationships, as well as through many future upheavals in our journey together. (See Appendix B for an explanation of the Enneagram.)

Connie, Rosanna, and I also all shared a love of reading and mutually thrilled to some of the new work emerging from theologians like Matthew Fox, who wrote, among other books, *Original Blessing: A Primer in Creation Spirituality*, and astrophysicists like Brian Swimme, author of many books that add a cosmic dimension to creation spirituality. I had long been reading as much of the new physics and cosmology as I could understand, because I always loved it when my worldview was broken open to something larger and more mysterious, more wonder-filled. The other two women each had their own particular spheres of interest. All three of us wanted our work on whatever front to be dynamic and always growing. We were committed together to the *big picture* in order to awaken our awe and gratitude for life and to cultivate our compassion for those who suffer around the world. Consequently, we were committed to working with women from any faith tradition or none, as I was learning to do with girls at Dana Hall, and we hoped to ground ourselves one day in a simpler, earth-based lifestyle.

One significant step along the way was coming up with a name for our evolving vision of work together, as well as for our dream of a potential retreat center. Having always been something of a wordsmith, a namer, I was the primary one on the lookout for this name. In time, it came to me through an old friend who was a trained spiritual director. She phoned to share with me a word that a woman she directed had given to a vision of the sacred she'd had in the woods one spring day as the sun poured through the trees: *Greenfire.* I loved the image and the word immediately, as did Connie and Rosanna when I told them about it. So Greenfire we became. Over the years, the name took on more and more associations, like with the burning bush in Exodus or with Hildegard of Bingen's *veriditas*, which referred to nature's divine healing, or *greening*, power. Eventually, we found the word showing up serendipitously in all kinds of places, even once as the title of an environmental protest song by a woman in Alaska.

Throughout this time, I was gradually discovering how much I longed, hungered, to move on from Dana Hall and work instead in the context of a small community of women, a sisterhood, a circle. However, both Jack and I were definitely thriving on many aspects of the Dana Hall chaplaincy and treasured our many deep friendships with folks in the school community. It had been a perfect job for me, and he was certainly not looking to move. But, in reality, my role was somewhat of an adjunct to the overall educational mission of the school, so there were lonely aspects to it for me. Many of my more administrative responsibilities—never my "sweet spot"—began to get old, as did the repetitious nature of the public prayers. Also, most of my ministry up to that point had been with young people—new young people every year, in fact. I discovered with my Greenfire sisters that I was missing the shared exploration of a more in-depth, mature spirituality. Once a desire like this takes root in me, I have trouble being patient with the process. But learning patience—and even learning to appreciate its practice—seems to be a big part of my work and of growing older.

As for the Greenfire dream, the circle idea was key all along. We explicitly wanted to move away from the male "Lone Ranger" model of ministry so prevalent across the board in most counseling and ministerial roles. So the three of us—as well as another priest, trained counselor, and friend, Alison Cheek, who joined us when she could—began envisioning and experimenting with how it would be to have two or three of us, instead of the traditional one-on-one, involved in a personal conversation with a woman. Connie knew many women at Wellesley College who were eager to experience such sessions with us and were willing to give us feedback on their time in lieu of paying us a fee.

Connie was also the one who came up with the idea of offering, along with individual sessions, what we came to call Work/Vision Consultations, in which three of us would meet with a woman for three sessions of two hours each. We would listen closely to the person's work or life questions and struggles, and then offer back to her what we were hearing so that she could hear herself more clearly and deeply. We considered dreams, used creative play and silence, gave homework, and soon began concluding the final session with a brief blessing ritual appropriate to the person and the outcome. Occasionally, we would feel that the process was floundering and leading nowhere, but most often the person would report significant insights along the way, and virtually everyone left with greater clarity and peace about her next steps.

In order to verify that our intuitions about our process were accurate, I interviewed several women who had worked with us. One woman, a psychologist and practicing counselor, launched right into her comments when we sat down together. "I have a couple of basic thoughts I want to note. First, it is a rare thing to be listened to—to have anyone wholly, fully allow you to have your voice and listen to you completely from a position of wanting the best for you. That's a true gift. And second, I've never been exposed to a mutual model before. You all have structured it so that it has to be mutual."

"What do you mean by that?" I asked.

"Well, to begin with, you disagreed with each other on various things. Plus you are each so fundamentally different that you modeled two things: One is that you all don't have the answer for me (it's impossible to combat that in therapy with one person), and the other is that I realized there isn't any *one* answer because each of you had a useful slice. Having all three of you there allowed each one of you to move more deeply into the thing you do best because you didn't have to worry about covering all the bases. You each remained fully the source of your own treasure and wisdom. That was so rich for me and put the accountability and ownership of what was right for me to do directly on me."

This woman's comments resonated with something we had come to feel. Having three of us together on a consultation allowed us each to touch that deep, intuitive, creative place inside ourselves. It allowed for ebb and flow, for the luxury of listening with a different ear because we weren't alone in holding this woman and her story. It soon seemed like a very natural, probably very ancient, thing for women to do—gather in a circle to hear and heal one another. It is also what indigenous peoples have been doing forever—circling up to listen attentively to one another in order to discern the wisest course of action.

Another woman I interviewed had been in an oppressive and abusive professional relationship. I began the interview by asking, "Could you say something about why you came to us?"

She replied, "When you said your model was women getting together to be for each other in the way that women have always done, that just sent chills through me—particularly the 'now it's my turn' thing. Especially for people like me who are caregivers, to have it be our turn has to be a really intentional thing."

I asked, "How did it feel when you then actually met with the three of us?"

"I really knew I needed help," she said. "But, had the reception I got from the three of you not been as it was, I would not have been so forthcoming. The quality of the reception that made such a difference is that *you heard me*—with no pity or encouragement to be strong. *You just heard me!* Then you gave me new ways of seeing what I was feeling. You validated and honored me...drew connections, gave me practical, spiritual, and psychological insights, helped me carry my thoughts further than I had been able to alone. The fact that you were able to hear and validate me without any judgment was probably one of the best things you did, probably the most Christ-like. You just accepted me as a person. That's what real friends do, but it's so rare and so needed!"

At one point I asked, "What was your experience of the three of us?"

She responded, "I could definitely see that the three of you knew each other well and weren't reluctant to talk or supplement each other. But it was always clear that what you were struggling to understand or express or deal with or whatever was totally *my* material."

"Did you experience us as offering different things?"

"I didn't see it that way at all," she said. "There was not any one particular bent that any one of you had. I experienced it all as just such a whole."

In another interview, a woman on the verge of bankruptcy and possible homelessness described her sense of the process. "I liked that you have three personalities and you all intuit in a slightly different way, so I just thought I was getting more. The atmosphere was helpful, too. It was casual, it felt soft, and I liked that we were physically close with a candle, rocks, crystals, flowers, and other interesting things around. I needed to come away from the world I left that morning. Being in the midst of all those treasures really enabled me to do that."

I then asked, "Can you say anything about what was not so great in the process?"

"Oh," she said, "I felt like I was in so much pain that I really missed a lot of it. But I felt like you really ministered to me in that. I wish I'd been able to do more, but you enabled me to do something that I had been trying to do for ten years: write a résumé. You all lovingly helped me do that. You gave me timelines and held me accountable, but so gently, assuring me that this wasn't a win/lose situation, that you'd be there for me. You also gave me language when I was stuck. And I did it! I actually did it. I wrote that résumé, and I don't think I would have done it without that process."

"We sure felt your pain during the sessions," I said.

"I felt that," she noted. "I knew you were all right there for me, holding me all the way."

Over time, the dream of doing more of this circle work together became clearer and stronger for the three of us, so we began seriously considering when and how we could leave our current jobs. In early 1989, Connie and Rosanna started researching potential settings and possibilities for a retreat center. Initially, they looked at properties within an hour or two of the greater Boston area, but these proved too expensive. Then, while visiting a friend in Tenants Harbor, Maine, they came across a charming little old New England farmhouse and phoned Jack and me with the news. They asked us to come see it immediately because they wanted to make an offer on it. We drove up the next day and could hardly believe it when we realized that Tenants Harbor was in the exact same area of midcoast Maine where we had twice vacationed and which we totally loved. We'd even briefly considered selling our Newton house and buying a getaway place there since we were living in campus housing. The serendipity of that geographical connection left Jack and me feeling that this farmhouse must be the place. So Connie and Rosanna purchased it that fall and immediately began renovations on the barn end to house retreatants, although they planned to continue their work lives in Boston for a year or two more.

Tenants Harbor was a lot further away from Jack's greater-Boston base of work than the properties Connie and Rosanna had initially been considering, so the obstacles to our joining them loomed even larger. Jack had at one time wanted us to move to Maine so that he could work with poor rural kids, but that was back when I was just being ordained and embarking on the chaplaincy ministry. By this point, Maine was no longer on his radar, and he couldn't imagine starting anew. In addition, our children were facing college expenses, so we needed all that my Dana Hall position offered financially, which, along with my modest salary, included free room and board on campus and a sizeable income from the rental of our Newton house.

I can so clearly remember my hunger for change and my feeling of being somewhat stuck during this time. I felt I needed something to enliven me during the intervening—possibly many—years before I might be free to leave my job and Jack might be ready to move. So I reconsidered an old dream of earning a doctorate. Fortunately, Dana Hall was supportive of its faculty pursuing continuing education. They not only allowed me to be gone for classes, they also provided some financial aid.

Initially, I considered sticking with my love of biblical theology and applying for a PhD program in Old Testament studies at Harvard, but I soon found myself much more drawn to the Doctor of Ministry (D.Min.) degree program in feminist liberation theology and ministry offered by the Episcopal Divinity School (EDS), then also in Cambridge. Similar to my attraction as an undergraduate to a major in humanities, I found myself still wanting to learn more about the historical roots of present-day patterns in hopes of finding clues for how to live more meaningfully and effectively into the future.

So with many concerns about juggling family, full-time work, and doctoral studies, I entered this D.Min. program. I soon found myself immersed in learning about the systemic nature of patriarchal oppression and the interconnection of all the isms—racism, classism, sexism, heterosexism, ableism, antisemitism, nationalism, militarism, and so forth. The eighties and early nineties was a dynamic time in the women's movement, as well as in the older Latin American movement of liberation theology with its passionate "preferential option for the poor." All kinds of books and other resources were pouring forth from these fronts, and it seemed as if my classmates and professors were all similarly on personal and communal journeys of awakening. I loved every bit of it!

For many white women, the only way we can begin to see and feel the effects of white privilege is to tune into our experience of male privilege. Many—if not most—of us were raised, unknowingly, to defer to male power. It became our default setting, even if we made a secret pact of equality with some man—like I did with Jack. Many of us discovered—as was true for me once I earned my Master of Divinity degree and got ordained—that even the credentials of educational and professional status don't really matter in the face of male privilege, especially white male privilege. Furthermore, almost every woman, whatever her age, race, class, or ethnicity, has had countless experiences of *mansplaining*, as well as experiences of her ideas not being heard until they are repeated later by some man. Dana Hall, with its predominantly female administration, offered me a break from these patterns. But they were quite obvious in the diocesan committees on which I agreed to serve, where it often seemed like all significant decisions were made behind the scenes by the men in power and were then just reported back to the committee as a whole. By the time I actually left Boston for rural Maine, I had begun to feel I had given my best self, my energy and ideas, my *babies*, away over and over again only to have them dismissed, dashed, or stolen. I was eager to work with women, but in a spiritual community.

One very significant dimension of the women's movement of the day was that Black and Hispanic women theologians were increasingly distinguishing their issues, as *womanists* and *mujeristas*, respectively, from those of white feminists. At the same time, many educated white women were still blind to the extent of their white, and often class, privilege. It is never easy to face one's own privilege and one's unconscious participation in racist, classist, or other systemic oppression. I remember an awakening I had at a major women's conference in the Boston area. It was announced that the small break-out groups would be separated by race or ethnicity, rather than mixed. While the Black and Hispanic women present seemed comfortable with this announcement, apparently many white women complained. One facilitator announced this reaction and asked, "What's the matter? Don't white women like white women?" For me the penny dropped as I thought to myself, *No, we don't. We tend to be kind of boring as a group, so we prefer to benefit from the soul power and passion of our sisters of color. Obviously we're still unconsciously using them to serve our lives and our needs!*

Meanwhile, as I was continuing on with my chaplaincy and doctoral work, we successfully incorporated Greenfire as a women's retreat center in Maine and secured nonprofit status. Our stated mission was to "serve the spiritual journeys of women from any faith tradition or from none." Then in June 1991, Connie and Rosanna left their Boston jobs and moved to Tenants Harbor full-time.

Jack and I, on the other hand, remained very much a part of the work and world of Dana Hall. However, difficult things had been unfolding for him in Young Life. He had decided to resign from the role of regional director because he and his staff in the New England region had developed an exciting team leadership model that they believed would make fuller use of peoples' gifts and better serve the region. This model would allow Jack to continue as part of the team but focus on his passion for urban ministry development and church relations. However, once Jack resigned, his boss used the opportunity to dissolve the team and replace Jack with someone from another region who didn't share Jack's vision for team leadership or for urban and church relations work.

Several years earlier, Jack had been given oversight of the work in Bermuda. Later, he was also asked to be Young Life's liaison with youth ministry in Ireland and the United Kingdom. He loved this work and the people he met overseas, quickly becoming a true Anglophile. I loved it all, too, those few times I was free to travel with him. Therefore, once he no longer had a regional role to play, Jack was free to become part of the International Department of Young Life, which excited him. He was also invited by the national Church-Relations Department to serve on their team. Shortly after he accepted those two roles, however, Young Life closed both departments in favor of a different organizational vision.

For Jack to lose one exciting avenue of work with Young Life after another was quite a blow and left him somewhat depressed. He couldn't imagine summoning the desire and energy to re-create his life and develop new work in Maine. I had promised him all along that I wouldn't move without him but would wait until he felt ready to move, too. So we were at a standstill for a time, although that served us well because I had my D.Min. classes to complete.

Gradually, though, Jack began to have a vision for potential work in Maine. He explored developing a small nonprofit called Youth Forum Maine (YFM), modeled on a very creative project called Youth Forum Minnesota, which had been started by my former Young Life leader and first boss, Phil McDonald. Through YFM, Jack could build a community team to connect caring adults with young people in a variety of settings in Maine, including with schools. He planned to focus on ministering to troubled kids, his old vision, while remaining on the Young Life staff for several more years because he had a strong base of financial supporters through that organization. So we were ready to begin looking at properties in Tenants Harbor and further imagining ourselves living there.

Chapter 10

Circling into Sisterhood

On my forty-ninth birthday, I decided to claim the following year as my Jubilee Year, after the ancient Hebrew tradition of proclaiming the seven-times-seventh year to be one of restoration and new beginnings. Everything came together. Jack launched YFM. We sold our Newton home. We purchased a simple little house on an ocean cove in Tenants Harbor, which we named Seafire. And we moved there in October 1992 on the weekend of my fiftieth birthday. Amy, Josh, and some of our friends helped with the move, and Connie and Rosanna treated us all to a birthday lobster feast at Greenfire. It was quite a Jubilee celebration!

Jack and I spent that school year commuting back and forth from Dana, where I worked part-time while Jack laid the groundwork for incorporating YFM as a nonprofit organization in Maine. We also remodeled Seafire, creating two small guest bedrooms and a guest sitting room out of two larger bedrooms to better accommodate our own family and guests or a couple of Greenfire retreatants. On every trip up from Boston, I delighted anew in the coastal views and increasingly rural quality of Maine along the way. Now this would be home! I could hardly believe the joy and wonder of this long-awaited move, of actually being able to wake up every morning to the sea air and changing tides. I enjoyed our close-in view of little islands and our long view of the ocean horizon, where occasionally we'd see large schooners, cruise ships, or transport ships passing in the distance. I thrilled to Maine's rugged, rocky coast and its forests of fir and other evergreen trees. And I loved our sun deck's private views of sunrises, sunsets, and the full moon over the water. (One magical summer night when I was home alone, I even danced naked on our deck under that full moon.) By June 1993, when we settled full-time into our little cove-side house, I felt like I'd come a long way from life in Wellesley, Massachusetts.

Although my paternal grandmother was from Maine, I never knew her, nor had I often visited the state. Still, I had a strong sense of soul-recognition, of coming home once we lived there. Then I read Kathleen Norris's book *Dakota: A Spiritual Geography*, in which she describes her connections to the Dakotan land of her ancestors. That was it. I felt Maine was somehow my *spiritual geography*. A few years later, when I visited my dear friend Gibbsie (Susan Gibbs) in Oslo, Norway, she drove me around the coast to Gothenburg, Sweden, from which my maternal great-grandparents had emigrated to the States. I could hardly believe how much that section of coastal Scandinavia resembled the Maine coast. Maybe my body, spirit, and soul had recognized its ancestral landscape, its spiritual geography.

However, even then I consciously knew that, no matter how much the Maine landscape mirrored that of Sweden and Norway, this was not the land of *my* ancestors. It is the land of the ancestors of coastal Maine's indigenous peoples, the nations that comprise the Wabanaki, or "People of the First Light." If I were to inhabit my adopted land soulfully, I needed to learn from and honor the wisdom of its peoples. Blessedly, in 2018 attorney, author, teacher, and activist Sherri Mitchell, a Wabanaki woman raised on the Penobscot Indian Reservation, whose name in her own tongue means "She Who Brings the Light," published *Sacred Instructions: Indigenous Wisdom for Living Spirit-Based Change*. It is a powerful book filled with historical perspectives and earth-based knowledge. It concludes with several prophecies that indigenous peoples from all over the globe asked Mitchell to share because they seem to point directly to these critical times. It is just what I had intuitively known I needed earlier, and it is just what we all need now because, according to Mitchell, everyone needs to be invited to the table if we are to work together to heal the earth—an archetypal Eris vision.

Although *The Uninvited Goddess* is about my journey, not Jack's, I want to note that our twenty-six-plus years in Maine have proved to be the most fertile and creative period of his life. He supported what was happening at Greenfire and initially even sat in on some of our circle gatherings and dinners. Several times, men asked for Work/Vision consultations, and Jack joined in on this circle work naturally and easily. He *got it* and became a much-loved extension of Greenfire. The real blessing, though, was that he soon became a much-loved member of the greater community. His ministry on behalf of young people and those who serve them has flourished and spun off in some amazing directions that now allow us to work together in wonderful ways—exactly as I had anticipated way back in seminary.

Once Connie, Rosanna, and I were all living in Tenants Harbor, we resumed the circle work we had begun in Boston. We had realized early on that doing personal-growth work in a circle, instead of one-on-one, would not be cost-effective. Our model was rather the emergence of something that would ultimately need to be developed further. As we said to one another, "Through us, the universe seems to be experimenting in using circles for this interpersonal inner work. That's our part, our offering. We are explorers of a new model. Other people will have to take it from here." We also knew there would be a lot more to learn individually and communally as we continued to explore our model.

We saw the whole Greenfire vision of a spiritual sisterhood working in circles as the culmination of our life's work and ministry. To gather in a circle was to put our bodies in the relationship of our vision. However, we were not looking to create an organization that would outlive us. We explicitly did not want financial considerations and long-term goals to dictate our decisions and direction. Rather, we wanted our intuitive responses to the work to guide us. We were able to consider this because, according to our calculations, each of our two households had sufficient resources to survive without real Greenfire salaries. Jack and I relied on his income, and Connie and Rosanna relied on such funds as pensions, Social Security, inheritances, and guest fees. We earnestly committed ourselves to a very simple lifestyle, which proved to be a hundred times easier in rural Maine than in Boston—and quite a relief to us all. Also, both Greenfire and YFM benefited from donations and small grants offered by friends and a couple of family foundations. I don't know if either nonprofit could have flourished without that initial generous and faithfully solid base of support.

For several years, we didn't know of anyone else exploring this kind of circle work or writing about it, but soon that started to happen. Many individuals or groups interested in starting their own retreat or circle ministry came to consult with us about our process, so the vision of circle work began spinning out from us. It was also springing up elsewhere. When Jean Shinoda Bolen's book, *The Millionth Circle: How to Change Ourselves and The World, The Essential Guide to Women's Circles*, came out in 1999, we said it was the book we should have written because it articulated all the things we did and taught. As the new science tells us, change doesn't usually proceed step-by-step, but rather through the sudden emergence of new models. Sometimes these emerge close together in time but in different locations. This is exactly what we experienced—and it was thrilling.

As I look back on the Greenfire years and all the things we attempted, learned, accomplished, or failed to accomplish, as well as all the people who came and went from our lives, teaching and changing us along the way, I find myself daunted by the task of telling the story. Much of it was miraculous, much was painful, and all of it was passionate, often playfully so. The early Greenfire story is recorded in quite a lot of detail in my doctoral thesis, *Greenfire—A Work in Progress: Reflections on the Story of an Emerging Feminist Liberation* Community, completed in 1995 then photocopied and widely distributed. But Greenfire went on until late 2007. By then, we had begun to make many of our decisions based on financial sustainability and growth—a departure from our initial vision. This evolution was the result of the popularity and success Greenfire enjoyed over the years and the committed investment of our devoted guests and board members. We were gratified to know that many people wanted Greenfire to outlive its founders, but the decision to do so changed everything. When it finally became obvious in 2007 that we were just too small to undertake the kind of capital campaign necessary to continue into the future, the board decided we should close. This was actually about the time we had always anticipated closing, but in a very different way.

So what went on during those years? First, individuals and groups who had met with us or heard about us in Boston came up to experience the retreat house. Guests would arrive saying something like, "Whoa, what a long drive…but I loved the quiet beauty of the woods and glimpses of the water all along the way."

They often couldn't wait to explore the area in more detail and would come back entranced. "I couldn't believe all the lobster boats in the harbors…with those picture-perfect coves and multicolored lobster buoys bouncing on the water everywhere I looked."

"I stopped for a lobster roll in the Port Clyde General Store. What a quaint and delightful place. They even had their woodstove going today to ward off the chill."

"There are so many great restaurants in Rockland…plus all those art galleries and fun shops. I love this area!"

At Greenfire we had a lovely rustic Great Room, as we called it, in the barn or retreat end of the farmhouse, and we soon began offering weekly evening meditation circles there for local women, followed by potluck suppers in our dining room. Women would arrive, leave their food offering in the kitchen, head down to the Great Room to join us and any guests present, then take one of our several meditation cushions and kneelers, a chair, or a spot on the rug, and we all gathered in a circle. There might be some chatting or kidding about what they had brought for the potluck, but soon one of us would sound our large crystal Tibetan singing bowl with a gong and a long drawn-out tone. Everyone would fall silent for twenty minutes until the bowl sounded again. Then we would talk together for another half hour or so about anything that had come up for anyone during the silence. These conversations might be about a remembered dream, an interesting book, a haunting question, a personal struggle, anything—light or heavy. One time when we were talking about how to respond to unwelcome requests for a visit, we came to the conclusion there was only one answer that was sure to work: "I'm sorry, but that's just impossible!" When it came time to hustle upstairs, set the table, and serve the food, camaraderie would break out—and friendships soon flourished.

We also offered Sunday morning worship circles in the Great Room. These evolved considerably over the years but eventually took a very simple shape, which included lots of silence, some readings or reflections, and the sharing of bread and juice. We would sit or kneel around a central altar-table, which typically held symbols of earth, air, fire, and water—for example, flowers in a vase of water, a lit candle, and a feather. After the opening thoughts and silence, a few words of invitation and welcome to the ritual meal were said—sometimes by one person, sometimes by all—to acknowledge the ancient sacred nature of shared meals, the essential oneness of creation, and gratitude for the presence of the Holy in our midst. Basically, we wanted to minimize words and allow the *action* of everyone partaking together around the table to speak for itself.

Our Greenfire accommodations were simple. We could house as many as five to eight people at the retreat house and two or three more in yurts that were built in our woods. We could house two more people at Seafire, which was luxurious by comparison but a couple of miles down the road. From the beginning, we supplied guests with breakfast and lunch fixings. On Wednesday through Saturday evenings, we served home-cooked, candlelit dinners in the Greenfire dining room, preceded by ten minutes of silent meditation. The circle-potluck gatherings provided dinner on Sundays, and if people were there on Mondays or Tuesdays, they were on their own for food.

Connie and Rosanna, who lived at the farmhouse and were definitely more extroverted than I, delighted in both cooking for and hosting our dinners. For the most part, too, they were more than happy to linger over the meal, enjoying the guests and the conversation—especially Connie, who was almost always the last person to leave the table. I, on the other hand, was more than ready to get going as soon as we finished eating because it had usually been a full day and I wanted to go home and relax with Jack. However, those of us who hadn't cooked (a rotating role) were responsible to assist the guests in cleaning up the kitchen after dinner. Unless I'd been the cook, I was in a quandary. Should I clean up the kitchen by myself? Interrupt the conversation to ask for help? Just go and leave everything in a mess? This continued to be a hard one to resolve because my life and introverted nature were so different from that of the others. In fact, the whole ministry of hospitality, which is of the essence of a retreat house, kept stretching me out of my comfort zone and into new growth. I loved our life in Maine, my Greenfire sisterhood, and the deeply contemplative circle work we were doing with guests, so I gave myself over to the more challenging hospitality aspects as well as I could.

The truth is that it was all of a piece and that each one of us was being stretched and challenged in different ways. For example, we soon recognized that the interpersonal tensions we faced were almost always rooted in our individual habitual patterns of *comparison, guilt, and blame*. Over and over again we faced these same issues. Over and over we struggled to spot them sooner so we could intervene, let go, and shift to our higher selves before wounds happened that then also needed to be healed. It was intense work. It dealt with our shadows, fears, inadequacies, anger, everything. It is work I still, and will probably always, need to do on myself at ever deeper levels, but what we learned from one another during the Greenfire years was life-altering.

We initially relied on word of mouth to spread the word about Greenfire, which worked amazingly well because we each had so many contacts. In early 1993, though, we began publishing a seasonal newsletter that we sent free of charge to guests, friends, relatives, and anyone who requested it. Through that means, we could advertise our retreat house and circle work as well as our workshops and special events, of which there were many over the years. We each wrote something for every issue, often reflections on local or current events or on what we were doing or learning. We also offered poems, recipes, book suggestions, photographs, and lovely drawings by neighbor Deborah Cotton, who soon became our design editor. For my introverted self, producing a written piece three or four times a year that would go out to practically everyone I knew was a challenge. As I was stretched by the demand, I grew. Eventually, I dared to offer poetic pieces from my extensive journal jottings. These were my most private musings and usually reflected my innermost thoughts, so it was a gift to have a place to offer them to others—and to find them well received.

After the shock of the attacks on September 11, 2001, we grappled with what to say in our upcoming fall newsletter. I ended up writing the lead article because of a dream in which I was supposed to preach a sermon on 9/11, but at the last minute found myself with nothing prepared. Unlike most such dreams, I was not at all concerned because I knew I just needed to lead a discussion and invite everyone to speak. I awoke with a calm, clear message: *We need to make space for all the voices, not just those up front and in power, to begin to address the crises facing our country and the world in new and potentially transformative ways, ways that will make a difference unto the seventh generation.* So I wrote about this dream and offered my thoughts for that newsletter. Then everyone else who usually contributed wrote their own reflections. In my piece, I noted that although public rhetoric seemed to promote a retaliatory "war on terrorism," I thought that would just play into the terrorists' hands, into their recruiting power. No one with whom I was in close contact thought that going to war was the answer. I heard, instead, an increasingly widespread groundswell of voices pleading for an exploration into the root causes of terrorism, pleading for a recognition of both the United States' arrogant complicity in the world's wounds and our overconsumption of the earth's bounty. What if, with a stance of repentant listening, we sought real dialogue and relationship instead of dominance? Wouldn't such actions ultimately better serve national security by rendering many of the ideologies that sustain terrorism irrelevant?

In looking back at that article for this chapter, I was startled to read the same concluding sentiments that I come to in this book, several years further along in the Era of Eris:

> We face an unprecedented opportunity to change our policies and ourselves in new yet simple ways that would be more in accord with our deepest religious values. We face the challenge to trust the creative Source that brought forth this whole risky human experiment—this earth-creature with such capacity for holiness and for destruction—and to discover that it is present in and interconnects the life-choice energy of each of us wherever it arises. We face the ever-present invitation to experience the reality that we are all one, one with our planet and the cosmos in an ever-changing dance of chaos and balance. With so many others, I pray for and seek to participate in the transforming movements of this dance!

We certainly experienced that "dance of chaos and balance" all along the way at Greenfire, as other women moved to the peninsula to join the inner circle of Connie, Rosanna, and me in the work: Adelaide Winstead, Connie's good friend and an original Greenfire board member; Maria Marta Aris-Paul, a Guatemalan priest; and Alison Cheek, the priest who had been part of our circle work in Boston and a co-founder. We also gradually needed to hire local women part-time to help us clean, cook, and manage the office. This put us in an awkward position of power imbalance. We were the *privileged* women *from away* doing the *deep, spiritual work*, while local women *served and cleaned up after us.* In an effort to address this, we asked one strong and insightful local woman to join our board and to speak her truth. That she did so and hung in there for several years was an incredible gift to us, though certainly not easy for her. We also invited onto our board some close friends who were women of color and soon found ourselves grappling with complex and personal issues of race as well as of class.

Decision-making at board meetings could be fraught. One of the tools we used to deal with particularly thorny issues was borrowed from indigenous peoples: a talking stick. We would pass our beautifully hand-decorated stick around and around the circle. Each woman who held it was able to express her thoughts without interruption or to pass until everyone felt satisfied and consensus had emerged. This unique process slows things down, creates time for real reflection, and allows adequate information and understanding to be shared. It is the opposite of patriarchal, top-down decision-making and seriously curtails manipulation by special interest groups. Instead, it builds trust and faith in community.

All of this meant that we founders were challenging ourselves and being challenged on all fronts as we floundered before the mystery of each other and our many interwoven issues. We always needed to raise more money, so we had to deal with our differences in that regard. We also had to face the difficulties caused by our positions of relative privilege and power in the concentric circles of involvement that were then Greenfire. Inevitably, each of us hurt others or was hurt along the way. It took all of our interpersonal gifts and accumulated wisdom to continue muddling along. We were grateful for books like *A Simpler Way*, by Margaret J. Wheatley and Myron

Kellner-Rogers, which offers insight into how life's organic processes for dealing with complexity suggest clues for cultivating vitality and creativity in human organizations. We occasionally hired consultants to help us sort out issues in our relationships. But mostly we just kept talking and processing amongst ourselves, using the familiar tool of the Enneagram and a new tool, astrology.

We all initially got interested in astrology in 1995 when Rosanna shared her taped reading by Arifa Boehler, one of the most gifted astrologers in Maine. It was so right-on to the Rosanna we knew and loved that each of us in the core circle then had a personal reading with Arifa, followed by several group consultations. She helped us understand more about our individual strengths and weaknesses, as well as how and where our differing balances of earth, air, fire, and water energies complemented and/or competed with each other.

In my reading, for example, Arifa informed me, "You have seven planets in air signs and a fire sign rising, which means that all the dynamic, fast-moving energies of air and fire are running the show. But your constricted earth-sign moon—the inner-mother, soul-container part of you—is crying out to slow down, simplify your life, and get grounded. In other words, you have no internal mother and are at risk of getting sick or something. You badly need to learn to mother yourself. While your decision to move to Maine was a definite beginning step, you still have a long way to go."

I knew she was right about my mother issues, of course—although precious few women, at least from my generation, have been well mothered because our mothers were not well mothered themselves. Still, I was not sure where she was going with this and asked, "What would that mean? How would I learn to *mother* myself?"

She replied, "You have to practice asking yourself basic good-mother questions: 'How do I feel? What do I need? What do I want?'"

"Okay..." I said, "but...I don't really get it...I mean, what should I *do*?"

And Arifa responded in no uncertain terms, "Nothing! Practice doing nothing. Just try relaxing...try sitting under a tree with a good novel and a box of bon-bons!"

Well, she certainly got my attention with all this, and I began focusing on self-mothering. But also, as is my wont, I started reading about astrology, studying with Arifa, and eventually offering to do readings for others, all of which I've been doing ever since. In brief, I would say now that astrology seems to function synchronistically in the sense explored by Jung of parallel phenomena that unfold into discernible patterns over time. One's birth chart is a map of the planetary archetypes as they appeared in the heavens at the moment of birth. Through this map one can get clues as to how these archetypes might be functioning intra-psychically and also what the soul's evolutionary path or work might be as the planets continue to move in orbit around the sun and touch on points of vulnerability. In other words, astrology can illuminate our transformative processes, relationship patterns, and soul journeys. It suggests that everything is connected and alive with meaning, that everything matters if received intuitively and imaginatively.

Astrology eventually led me to Eris. The bulk of my air energy—Sun and four planets—is in the astrological sign of Libra, symbolized by the cosmic scales of Justice. From the beginning, Libra's passion for beauty, relationships, balance, paradox—light and dark, shadow and hope—was quite familiar. I have always delighted in being stretched through and beyond paradox into the unknown, into the places where boxes break down and mystery abounds, where the mind is freest to roam. However, Libra has long been trivialized as the light, bright, superficial, indecisive, somewhat lazy face of the feminine. But it is the cardinal air sign, opposite the cardinal fire sign of Aries, which is ruled by Mars and signifies ego consciousness and masculine drive. Therefore, Libra must hold the opposing full and vital force of collective consciousness and the feminine. It must be about awakening both to the Other and to our essential oneness with all beings, the earth, and the cosmos.

Fairly soon, I began feeling that Libra's strong cardinal power and breadth of balance—its reputed iron fist in a velvet glove—was underrepresented by gentle, beauty-loving Venus as its ruling planet. In some astrological circles, the search for an as-yet-unknown but long-suspected tenth planet, Planet X, which might prove to be the more comprehensive ruler of Libra, was being talked about, and that excited me. When I learned in 2005 about the discovery of a Planet X, nicknamed Xena by her discoverers after the fictional warrior princess, I was hooked! My avid interest in this new planetary archetype, eventually named Eris and generally accepted as the ruler of Libra, grew and deepened the more I learned. As described in the Prologue, it all led eventually to this book.

While my journey with Eris took place beyond and outside of Greenfire, what we learned about astrology greatly aided us in our personal growth and interpersonal struggles. Thankfully, though, our guests seemed to appreciate the fact that life at Greenfire was not always neat and pretty, but pretty real—and sometimes raw. Since we were small and our accommodations were tiny and somewhat intimate, I think guests came to feel they were part of our greater family. They and the whole local community of women who gathered round us offered more love, support, and understanding than I can describe. They kept us honest and on path. For our part, we were living our dream and constantly being stimulated and enlivened by the creativity, depth, and growth the work both demanded and offered.

We also developed several practices that helped to sustain us over the years. Those of us who primarily did the circle work of conversations or Work/Vision consultations continued to meet together weekly in our own core circle for silence and sharing, as we had done since we began in Boston. This gathering initially included Connie, Rosanna, and myself. Adelaide joined us once she arrived, and Maria Marta and Alison took part whenever they could.

At one of these early circles, we talked about our evolving understanding of the priesthood. Rosanna made a statement that resonated with my whole journey into and through ordination and that has stayed with me ever since. She said, "The work of a priest is to *make space* for the Holy and *not to fill it.*" This I always knew I wanted to do—to find or create open space for mystery and guidance, to hang out in the unknown, and to be met there however it happened, both individually and communally. All too often it seems, worship services leave no silence and precious little space for inspiration, for the Holy. I think people go to services hoping for that sacred encounter but satisfy themselves instead with a sense of community. My longing for deeper work with women was a longing to open up this space and to dwell more fully in it.

Those of us doing the circle work, and any others who wanted to join, were certainly being held by our participation in the Sunday morning worship circles, the weekly evening meditation circles, and the ten minutes of silence before dinner. Early in the evolution of Greenfire, we also began closing the place to guests for up to a week every fall, winter, and spring for our own silent retreats because we realized that we had brought our busy overachiever selves with us from Boston. In order to slow down and run a retreat center, *we* had to practice going on retreat and into silence ourselves. Jack always participated in these retreats, too, and they became so delicious and significant for both of us that we still try to set aside such blocks of time.

There is more and more awareness these days of how rarely any of us is actually in the present moment instead of following our overactive and impatient minds back to the past or into the future. And there is increasing awareness of the possibility of *flow*, that delicious sense of participating naturally, even communally, in an unfolding present. In their best-selling book *Stealing Fire: How Silicon Valley, the Navy SEALS, and Maverick Scientists Are Revolutionizing the Way We Live and Work*, authors Steven Kotler and Jamie Wheal examine contemporary explorations of flow. They describe the experience as having four characteristics: *selflessness, timelessness, effortlessness,* and *richness.* They also demonstrate that, while it is human nature to seek these feelings, they can become addictive as well as manipulated for military or commercial purposes. Maturity and wisdom are needed to maintain grounding in ordinary life. As Buddhist teacher Jack Kornfield put it in the title of one of his books, *After the Ecstasy, the Laundry.*

At Greenfire, we learned about and practiced many models of meditation and spirituality while always seeking to remain grounded. I was particularly drawn to Zen Buddhism, which assumes that enlightenment or awakening is the natural state of mind in all sentient beings, and that one's work is to accept—live into—that reality. Several of us also loved working with the chakras and other practices that are based in bodily awareness. We made altars for all our gatherings, as well as in our private meditation spaces, using art, flowers, stones, sea glass, driftwood, Christian or goddess images, pictures, symbols, books—anything that spoke to us of the earth, the divine, and the feminine. Many of our guests were inspired to create their own meditation spaces and altars when they returned home and would later tell us how meaningful that was.

Looking back on this whole period of my life, I remember how daring and freeing it felt to *play* with language and symbols in ways that would have been taboo in the more conservative Christian circles of Young Life in which I had been nurtured. I wrote poetry for the goddess in her various guises and felt more whole, like a part of myself was being reclaimed and honored. These days, I find myself drawn to the simplicity of silence and nature rather than to ritual and images, but these were crucial and life-giving steps along the way. Many women have to find and live into their *wilder* selves in order to break the bonds of old conditioning—in order to liberate their power, voice, and creativity. Perhaps that was part of the magic of Greenfire. We were on this journey ourselves and simply inviting others to join us.

At first, most of our guests were from the Boston area, but increasingly they came from Maine and all of New England. Soon we started attracting a steady stream from California and elsewhere around the country. We would say to the women from California and other far-off places in the States, "Surely there must be something like us nearer home for you!" But they would say in effect, "No, you are truly unique. We can't get this anywhere else!" We also drew people from many other countries, including Canada, New Zealand, Australia, Greece, and Germany. Several of the youth workers from the United Kingdom and Ireland with whom Jack and I worked via Young Life also came to Greenfire over the years, usually for a retreat and Work/Vision consultation.

Offering space for women to pay attention to their inner selves set the stage for each of us to do the same. I remember one time when we asked a woman to facilitate such experiences for us, I sensed or heard my inner voice say, *I want to sink my roots deep into the earth and spend more time there!* It was a previously unknown longing that I nonetheless knew, from both astrology and the Enneagram, I should heed.

Another such awakening occurred one New Year's Eve when a small group of local women came together at Greenfire to reflect on what we were being led to explore in the coming year. One close friend, who happens to share my Enneagram type, told us, "When I began asking myself where I was being led, I suddenly heard my inner voice exclaim, 'I am an artist!'" The minute she said that, my inner voice said, *And I am a contemplative!* It was a deep, private moment, but over time, when I've sought guidance for the work I should be focusing on, especially once Greenfire closed, that is the calling I hear. Such is the power of our inner voices. When we can honor them as healthy and spiritually true, they are lifelong guides.

A third experience occurred not long after 9/11. I came awake in the night thinking about a local project that was closing and wondering dreamily about fields of information—about what happens to information that was on the web after a website is closed. That led me to think about how the new science views quantum-level interacting fields of information, and I suddenly thought, *There is a field of peace, in which the Dalai Lama and other peacemakers live, and there is a field of war, which is dominating much of human consciousness.* Then I heard my inner voice say, *Find the field of peace and learn to live there!* It was as strong an inner voice as I've ever experienced, and it has influenced my life and inner work ever since. I want to radiate an inner journey to peace in all that I say and do, as opposed to the fear-based defensiveness and aggression emanating from so many fronts these days. It is a conviction expressed most eloquently by Etty Hillesum in *An Interrupted Life*: "Ultimately, we have just one moral duty: to reclaim large areas of peace in ourselves…and to reflect it toward others. And the more peace there is in us, the more peace there will also be in our troubled world." She wrote this diary entry in support of people she knew who were being herded off to Auschwitz on September 29, 1942—not long before her death and just eight days before my birth into grief and this grieving world.

I am so grateful for these inner-voice experiences, as well as for the fact that I lived and worked in a community that valued intuitive guidance and therefore encouraged me to pay attention to such times. I think everyone has access to inner guidance in one form or another, and I believe it is absolutely critical to the human community that in both small settings and large we encourage and support one another in tuning in to that guidance. We are each uniquely gifted and needed. Furthermore, as Jung helped us see, we have more to guide us than just our inner resources because synchronicities abound around us. Our work is in learning to notice and increasingly trust such signs, such guidance. This level of discernment can make all the difference to the sense of becoming more fully oneself and doing the work that expresses that self. Most especially, though, it offers hope for our world.

Over time, the idea of Greenfire's long-term survival took root—even as financial issues loomed. For one thing, the property increasingly needed a lot of work, but it was hard to raise money for this while it was still privately owned. It became increasingly obvious that, were we to continue, we would need to have a capital campaign to raise enough money for the board to buy the property from Connie and Rosanna, as well as enough money to maintain the place and hire the support staff required for the ongoing ministry. The board eventually voted to explore this path, and we all had even more to do.

Meanwhile, on the personal front, Connie and Rosanna's relationship had become quite strained, and they eventually separated. In 2002, Rosanna decided to follow an old yearning to live in the Southwest and moved to Arizona, where she has had a fulfilling life and ministry ever since, complete with a lovely new partner. At some point, both Maria Marta and Alison also moved away for their own personal reasons. And Connie found a new partner, who moved into Greenfire and quickly got involved in all aspects of our life there. Much as she loved Greenfire, though, she did not share the vision for and commitment to the kind of inner, circle work that had brought the rest of us there in the first place. The strain of differing personalities and agendas, as well as of financial needs, increased.

It seems, in retrospect, that we at Greenfire were making some big decisions about our long-term future at the same time as we were losing founding members who had shared a common vision. I would say, paraphrasing a line from Yeats's poem "The Second Coming," that "things were falling apart; our center could no longer hold." Too many of us found ourselves operating at cross purposes, unable to discern how to transform our founding vision into the new agenda. For my part, I was more than willing to continue with the circle work, but less willing, at that age and stage of life, to give myself to the countless highly stressful administrative tasks necessary to build an ongoing organization.

As Jack approached seventy and I approached sixty-five, which was around the time we all had originally envisioned Greenfire slowing down, I tried to figure how I could free myself up to share more of life and ministry with Jack in a way that would simultaneously benefit Greenfire. The board was clear that a strong capital campaign would depend on solid long-term staffing. I didn't want to make a commitment beyond participation in the circle work, whereas Connie, the only other paid circle worker, wanted to stay fully involved. Plus, she owned and lived on the property. So, in mid-2005, I offered to leave the staff the following June to contribute my small pay-line to the possibility of hiring a full-time person. I also offered to keep doing the circle work as a volunteer as much as I could for as long as I was needed. The board received this offer most graciously and initiated a mini-campaign to fund *two* full-time staff women to replace me, a move they hoped would ready us for a real capital campaign.

Following a search and Connie's recommendations, the board hired two mature and gifted women who had often visited Greenfire, and they each moved to the area in mid-2006. Sadly, though, things did not work out well—either for Connie or for them—and they left the staff within their first year. Fortunately, they each went on to develop fulfilling lives here in Maine, but Greenfire did not survive the upheaval. For several months, Connie tried to convince the board that the work could go on with some very gifted part-time women she had found. But that was not to be. Our revenues kept shrinking, and in August 2007, the board voted unanimously to close the retreat center that November. Everyone agreed that it was better to end while we were still well regarded than to peter out gradually. Our closing was accomplished with great care under the wise guidance of a very committed local board member. We served well the guests who came in the interim, wrapped up all the legal and financial details, distributed fairly the many material things we had accumulated, and concluded with a big celebration of Greenfire's many wonderful years.

This Greenfire story is not unlike that of many visionary projects that have trouble adapting to change and moving beyond the founder stage. Some do it successfully, with or without making major shifts in vision. Others, like Greenfire, close down. The fact is that change is inevitable—and change is difficult! Knowing where flexibility is needed versus where continuity should prevail is also difficult. How many marriages, projects, communities, even countries fall apart over such issues! The awakening for me as I reflect on all this is how complicated each person is and how hard it can be to stay in community even after years of doing good and loving work together and even with the best intentions. Deep and abiding grace are necessary to endure the pain of change and loss long enough to create a container large enough to hold new and unfolding realities in some kind of communal vision. In this new era of the twenty-first century, we are facing this challenge on a global scale.

I was writing the initial draft of this Greenfire chapter from late March through early May 2018. On the second of April that year, while returning from visiting her daughters and their families in Boston for Easter Sunday, Connie was killed in a tragic car accident. This sudden loss of my longtime soul sister hardly seemed real for months. Connie's daughters asked me to share remembrances of her role in the Greenfire story at her memorial service, so I prepared that talk even as I was grappling with her death and trying to describe those years in this book.

Connie had gone to Boston that weekend instead of having her daughters come to Maine because on Saturday she, along with Jack and I, had attended the memorial service of my dear friend and long-time Greenfire board member Esu Lackey. That service drew a crowd of former Greenfire friends, staff, guests, and board members, and Connie loved every minute of seeing and talking with them all. Her memorial service in Maine just three weeks later drew an even larger Greenfire crowd. It was strikingly synchronistic to experience the positive energy and wonderful shared memories of Greenfire with these many folks just as I was attempting to write about it all. I had been sitting at my desk in my little corner of Maine trying to dredge up the full story when it was suddenly enfleshed and surrounding me in loving and grieving community during the two services. It is abundantly clear that Greenfire continues on in the lives of countless people who passed through over the years, and I treasure the thought that Connie tasted that at Esu's memorial service just two days before her death.

Chapter 11

Contemplating Life

As the end of my employment time at Greenfire drew near, Jack and I considered a move from Tenants Harbor to Rockland, the town at the head of the peninsula. The taxes on our waterfront property were rising. Three of our adult children lived in Rockland or neighboring Rockport with their children and needed more support. And Jack had to go into town almost daily for his various ministries. We stumbled upon a sweet two-hundred-year-old, somewhat-remodeled Cape and bought it in 2005. We dubbed the new place *Crossroads* because of its handy location, and it quickly became a gathering space for us all. That blessed little Cape was sunny and well laid-out, with a large family room/kitchen area, a first-floor master bedroom suite, three guest bedrooms and a full bath upstairs, a large garage office for Jack, lovely writing spaces for me, and a huge sweeping lawn on which the grandchildren could play.

A few years earlier, Josh had bought a wooded double lot on Cargill Pond in Liberty, a little over half an hour's drive from Rockland, and we bought the neighboring single lot. We so enjoyed camping there the first summer that, when a triple lot on the other side of Josh's became available, we bought it and sold our single lot to Amy, who wanted in on this family dream. Then in 2003, Jack and I decided that, since it would be years, if ever, before our children could afford to build, we would build a modest year-round family cottage on our land. It seemed to us that the best gift we could give to our grandchildren, as well as the best investment we could make on their behalf, would be to create a place that would allow them to spend lots of time in the Maine woods by this pristine and beautiful pond. We have never regretted that decision. It has been a healing spot for us all at various times, and having it lessened the loss of Seafire when we moved. It has also served over the years as a blessed retreat space for several friends and youth workers.

Although we have missed our many friends and the unique beauty of Tenants Harbor, living in Rockland has allowed Jack and me to more easily get involved in the lives of our children and grandchildren whenever they need us—for support, child care, rides, or whatever. What a challenge and a gift it has been that, apart from John David, we all now share much of life together. We can help one another out, grapple amongst ourselves with the residue of our family history, learn from one another's many gifts and struggles, and celebrate family events, holidays, and life's turning points together.

In 2015, we all celebrated Jack's and my fiftieth wedding anniversary, which still seems hardly possible because, at the time of our marriage, we would never have aspired to fifty years together. Not only did we not then know anyone who had been married that long, we hardly knew anyone who had lived that long! Now here we were, still gratefully together and relatively healthy, going for life and the long haul. The festivities took place at our lakeside cottage in Liberty. All the kids, grandkids, significant others, and our nephew and his family were there, along with Peter Edwards, the priest from our parish, and his wife. The big surprise was that my brother David and his wife, Margaret, from Wisconsin also showed up! Jack and I had put together a little ritual of blessing, which Peter led. People offered thoughts or remembrances, Jordan, our oldest granddaughter, sang "A Wedding Blessing," and the other four granddaughters sang "Can't Help Falling in Love." We shared an amazing feast that the kids all prepared, and then Jack and I went off to enjoy several days with David and Margaret.

Shortly after we moved to town, I experienced another awakening in the context of healing my physical body. I had consulted with a wise local physician who specialized in homeopathic medicine to help deal with an enlarged parathyroid gland that was inhibiting calcium absorption. Under his guidance, I did a lot of meditative work on my throat chakra. In the process, I realized I had long had a dull ache there, which upon reflection felt as if it had come either from too much crying or from holding back tears. As I sat with this feeling, I got an image of a crying baby in me, a baby who was forever wailing to be held and fed—or who had cried herself out and given up. She seemed to reveal the roots of my long eating disorder—she was starving for mothering and milk. She also seemed to reflect the fact that I am still rarely free enough to cry. I always knew I had made an early childhood decision not to let Mom see me cry, not to let her see that she had hurt me. But this image of the baby helped explain a lot more.

Over the years, my crying inhibition had become a real handicap to showing my genuine feelings. For example, when Jack and I were first dating, he, not me, would be the one who cried at movies—much as I tried to squeeze out a few tears. Ever since, I've wanted my throat, my feelings, and my voice to be more fully free. So I made a promise to this inner baby that I would hold and listen to her always. In the end, I did have surgery on that parathyroid gland, but what I learned along the way was more than worth it. This work of finding, listening to, and comforting our injured inner child of whatever age can be incredibly freeing. Many people with whom I've shared this story have told me so and shared their stories in return.

In 2008, one of the most momentous events in our lives took place—the candidacy and eventual election of Barack Obama as President of the United States. It was all unbelievably exciting to so many of us—his thoughtful style, his moving message of hope and change, his grassroots support base, and, of course, his race, his brilliant and equally eloquent wife, and his two lovely daughters. Both Jack and I were raised as Republicans, but we had long since become Democrats because of our humanitarian commitments. During the Bush years, I had registered with the Green Party because I wanted to take a stand with what I most deeply believe, having become totally frustrated with both major parties. I switched back, though, in order to vote for Obama in the Democratic primary—although it was hard to imagine that a Black man really would be voted in as President.

Jack and I went to a party the night of the election, and when we returned we found several phone messages from daughter Anna.

First: "Hey, where are you two? Can you believe this?" Then: "I have to talk to you! Where are you? This is fucking unbelievable. He actually might win!" And finally: "Holy shit!! It happened. Obama is going to be President!"

The next morning her daughter Jordan, then almost thirteen, asked her, "Mom, you're half Black, right?" When Anna answered that she was, Jordan proudly proclaimed, "That makes me one-quarter Black!" Such life-altering healing and joy all around—globally, as it turned out, for a while.

Most of us who were excited about Obama's hope for change were frustrated by the Republican Party's opposition to anything he tried to do. Reportedly, several key figures vowed they would take the country down before they would grant him any victory. Nothing is simple, but it seems they did succeed in bringing the country to a stalemate—despite the fact that Obama eventually was reelected, claimed his power, and enacted some, in my opinion, important and needed changes. During his presidency, though, many divisions in this country deepened, as did the anger and frustration of those who, for many valid reasons, felt displaced and unheard by the political establishment—those who felt *uninvited to the party*. This polarization has now become global and is a clear hallmark of this Era of Eris. We are all in trouble and desperately need to find our deeper, truer selves.

Since Greenfire closed, I've been able to focus on my sense of calling to the more contemplative, inner path. I've worked on my meditative writing and published a book of 365 poetic offerings. I've also worked on learning to quiet the *monkey mind* and to abide in *the field of peace*, as once directed by my inner voice. Thankfully, as West has increasingly met East, wisdom tools abound. For 2,500 years, for example, Buddhism has been exploring the workings of the mind. It can offer the rest of us better access to our more mystical intuitions through training in meditation and contemplation. It can teach us to hold suffering through transformative practices like *tonglen*, where one learns to breathe in pain and breathe back out happiness. We've even come to the point nowadays where scientists who study consciousness and the brain are meeting with the Dalai Lama to exchange notes.

Although I confess that I've resisted strict self-discipline most of my life—possibly a result of all the rigid diets I tried but ultimately failed to follow—I did begin to meditate more regularly and wrote my own Daily Office of short affirmations of intention and gratitude to be offered at specific times throughout the day and evening. (This is included in Appendix C for anyone interested in following the practice or writing their own.) Learning to pay attention, in the present, to the body and the breath helps one to become more grounded and to create more space and quiet internally for the sake of a more wholesome life. Another helpful tool is Buddhist teacher Pema Chodron's simple recommendation to pause, to *create a gap* for two or three breaths throughout the day, as a way to make present the spaciousness of mind one might—or might not—experience in more formal meditation sessions. Through such practices, we Westerners can learn over time to loosen the relentless grip of our rational, discursive minds with their need to know, their need for facts and conclusions. We can learn instead to relax into the territory of not-knowing, of silence, inner peace, and guidance.

With the ending of Greenfire, I discovered that the long break from the language and theology of the Episcopal church service had released me from reacting so much to its patriarchal style. I could choose to attend church on Sunday mornings with ever-faithful Jack and simply appreciate the sacred intention of the ritual gathering, the people themselves, and the gospel narratives—Jesus's commitment to the poor and marginalized, his faithfulness to truth and justice in the face of oppressive systems, his recasting of traditional laws for the sake of human needs, his healing powers, his enigmatic and wise parables, and his prioritization of love. I could also choose to stay at home and have a delicious meditative morning alone.

My fairly introverted nature has often led to more solitary pursuits and choices, which have at times left me feeling a little lost in our highly extroverted culture, dynamics explored by Susan Cain in her book, *Quiet: The Power of Introverts in a World That Can't Stop Talking*. The truth is that these introverted predilections, plus my love of reading and entering the liminal space of fantasy and imagination, may have facilitated experiences of awakening and flow. Of course extroverts have all these capacities, too, and they certainly experience times of enforced solitude and suffering that can open inner doors. Also, most extroverts allow themselves to explore their more introverted side as they mature. Spirituality in some form or another seems to be an innate capacity of every human being. However, it is usually up to us to cultivate it.

It is also up to us to recognize the devastating divisiveness within, between, and among the world's religions and to find creative, healing ways to respond. We conscious human creatures desperately need something big enough to work on that it will bring us together—such as saving life on this planet! We need to discover and learn to live from our compassionate hearts, which the spirit and wisdom of our religions' founders, prophets, teachers, and stories may yet help us to do. I think, for example, of the Christian mystics' teachings about oneness and love and the Buddhist vision that all beings be free from suffering and enjoy happiness. I find hope in the perspective that the uninvited Eris archetype gives us: Everyone needs to be included or there will be trouble—everyone needs a place at the table if we are to discern how to save the planet. And *everyone* means one hundred percent of the human family, the so-called *good* and the *bad* together. In other words, we will need to understand that we *all* belong here on this planet, that we are all ultimately One, and that we all long at some level for connection and communion with and through the same divine reality. There are many, many names for this reality, but all too often these names have proven divisive instead of unifying. I am more and more comfortable with wordlessness these days. However, we human beings *need* words, ones that aren't divisive and don't carry too many religious overtones. Perhaps scientific language will increasingly suggest possibilities. I think of the phrase *underlying field of consciousness*.

A tool that has recently become meaningful and helpful to my vision of our individual and corporate spiritual journey is the work of the nonprofit HeartMath Institute. According to its website, since 1991 this organization has "researched and developed reliable, scientifically based tools to help people bridge the connection between their hearts and minds and deepen their connection with the hearts of others." They demonstrate scientifically that the magnetic field of the heart is much more powerful than that of the brain, that emotional and other impulses actually originate in the heart before the brain, and that people can learn to bring their hearts, brains, and autonomic nervous systems into greater coherence—into a more stable and balanced rhythm—using heart-focused breath and positive thoughts. This coherence enhances all bodily functions, which in turn increases intuitive access, or *flow*, and positively influences those around us and our connections with them. In other words, we are beginning to understand scientifically that balance between our hearts and our brains, between the more traditionally understood feminine and masculine sides of ourselves, is essential to overall health and well-being, not just individually but collectively. The HeartMath initiative is also studying the *earth's* magnetic fields to discover how *human* energetic fields might affect the *global* field environment in order to find out if it would be possible to raise the vibrations of our collective consciousness for greater kindness and cooperation—potentially such significant and needed work.

I've continued to study, forever at a beginner level, what is being learned in the physical sciences and in the field of consciousness about the dynamics and power of thought itself. We know now that matter *matters*! When things *matter* to us, they become more real. They take on heft and presence. Yet, as scientists tell us, matter is essentially energy *bleeping* or vibrating into and out of form, depending on our observations of it. So matter and energy or spirit are two sides of the same coin. We observe *things* as matter and *space* as empty, but all of it is full of energy, being, potentiality. And it is all interconnected "non-locally," as science puts it, across space and time, although space/time ceases to have its familiar linearity and distance at the quantum level. So we perceive things into solidity, not just through our visual perception but through all of our senses as we live from day to day. And that's a wonder-filled truth. To use a familiar phrase from *The Book of Common Prayer*, "this fragile earth, our island home" is an unbelievably beautiful place, spinning its way around our modest life-giving star that dances along on a far-flung arm of the Milky Way, our stunning spiral galaxy, which is but one of an estimated two hundred billion to two trillion galaxies, *each* with billions of stars, in the unimaginably marvelous and mysterious observable universe. Now, that's a story!

Furthermore, we are not imprisoned here on earth by our physicality and sensory perceptions. The energetic vibrations of neurons in our brains line up, resonate, or sync with one another to facilitate types of consciousness—and we can learn to influence that process. When we cultivate our contemplative capacities through training and practice, we begin to sense the oneness of all people and things and perhaps even perceive something of the beauty and glory that pervades all that is. We have the innate capacity to abide ever more fully in the awareness of presence, emptiness, love—to flow with events and hold both suffering and joy. As we become less reactive to external circumstances, we become more compassionate and grateful people.

In this life, we always function as bodies—physical, beautiful bodies—but our bodies are also potential bridges to spirit, essence, energy. The atoms of every single creature and thing were made in the explosions of stars. We are stardust, and our auras all glow with emanated energy—no need for the glitter of gold or jewels. In light of the oneness of spirit/matter and the consciousness that undergirds it all and in which we participate, it can be said that we are ensouled flesh in an ensouled cosmos.

But we are in big trouble here on Mother Earth. We are all awakening to the reality of climate change, air and water pollution, the proliferation of toxic waste, the gradual extinction of species, and so forth. To the horror of many of us, we seem to have become the plastic-making species, turning our earth into a plastic planet with islands of plastic trash forming in our oceans. True spirituality has always invited us, in Martin Buber's words, to move from an *I–It* relationship to creation back to an *I–Thou* relationship, as exemplified by indigenous peoples. According to many of their elders in the Americas and other lands, the earth is desperately calling to us to *pay attention* to what is going on—calling us to love her back and help heal her.

So my focus in recent years has been to read and meditate/breathe, however irregularly, to share in Jack's work and in the lives of our families and many friends, and to try to stay somewhat current on global events, offering my heart and voice in service of a better world. A few years ago, I began wishing we could downsize to further simplify our lives and free up our aging energy. With all of our children but John David in the area, we were using their homes more and more for family gatherings, rather than Crossroads. And most people who came to visit us preferred to stay at our lakeside cottage.

Since we have a commitment to the family to maintain that cottage as long as possible, it increasingly seemed too much to care for a family home in town, too. Although Jack has been in great health, he was nearing eighty, and I didn't want to wait till he, or I, was no longer physically able to help with a move. At our age, you think about these things because you have so many reminders of mortality as friends and family members become infirm or seriously ill.

We eventually found and quite liked a lovely cottage in a small retirement community in Rockland—the Stonewood Road Cooperative. We sold Crossroads and moved in time for Jack's eightieth birthday. In the process, I reviewed and burned all my journals because I felt that the best bits were in my book of poetic offerings and no one needed to see the rest. Together, Jack and I cleared out a lifetime of accumulated *stuff*. We gave countless things to our children and grandchildren, sold what we could, and donated the remainder. All in all, it was an arduous but satisfying move that has greatly simplified our lives. I think, too, that it actually freed up my energy for the experience of my epiphany dream, described in the Prologue, and the subsequent writing of this book.

With the move, Jack and I have also reopened the possibility of living intentionally in community as we try to care for and support our mostly even-more-elderly neighbors. Community living is always challenging. All one's lingering issues can be triggered in tense or tiring situations, as I recently experienced at a meeting of our co-op board. People's experiences or perspectives differ widely, and health, age, or hearing loss issues can make dialogue difficult. The situation brought back memories of difficult times and interactions at Greenfire. I am discovering anew how much I still need to work on—even as I am becoming more aware of the urgent need for this on so many fronts in the world.

I've long known through Enneagram work that my ego-identity is in part about being a big-picture, fairly objective observer who sometimes sees what's going on when others fail to do so. The problem is that while our ego-identity is usually mixed up with and reflects true gifts and abilities, it is also our biggest problem and the barrier to our deeper selves. Our gifts are no help—and can definitely make things worse—if we are unaware that we have been triggered and are operating out of ego. Sometimes when I get hooked, I respond by withdrawing and going inward, tense and afraid of the potential repercussions of confronting the situation. Sometimes, impatient and irritated, I speak out too quickly, trying to get everyone on the same page—all too often, *my* page.

For any of us, when we recognize that we are being triggered, we can remember that everyone sees through their own lens and that the offerings of everyone at the table are needed to come to the best results. Then we can freely choose whether or when to offer our perspectives, to speak our truth. Sometimes speaking truth takes great courage. Always it demands thoughtfulness and kindness. Personally, nowadays I just try to take deep breaths, center myself, listen carefully, and seek intuitive guidance about when to be silent, when to speak, and what to say to offer my piece of the puzzle. All the while, I seek to remain hopeful on the local—and every—front that, as more of us do more of the same, wisdom will gradually emerge.

To conclude the "My Stories" part of this book, I want to note that I am grateful beyond words for fleeting experiences of Presence, oneness—of sensing the holiness in all things and trusting that consciousness undergirds the whole show from quantum particles to the farthest galaxies and background fields. I'm also grateful to have learned a bit about how to drop down and into the ever-present field of peace and wellspring of compassion holding us all. And I am grateful to know that essentially it is all about *being*, not *doing*—about awareness, waking up to here and now and living life gratefully and fully from there.

If someone were to ask for a summary of my awakenings, I would say this: I looked for the missing key to the meaning of life and found, or was found by, God, the Holy, the Christ, my Higher Power, Mystery, Love, Consciousness itself. I looked for a reason to become a priest and awakened to a calling to feminist liberation work of all kinds. I looked for community and found it over the years with other youth workers, with those working at Dana Hall School for Girls, with the vision and work of my Greenfire sisters, and now, perhaps, with a little community of elderly folks. I looked for an archetype to carry my full, Libran passion as a woman warrior for justice and found Eris—or She found me! I sought to become a contemplative and am finding Presence, the field of peace, in the gaps, in the Now.

If asked how I see Christianity these days, I would say that the gospel narratives of Jesus, the reality that love is stronger than death, and the presence of the Spirit in all beings and things are the root and core of my life. They were the essence of my early conversion experience to Jesus and God as the missing key to the meaning of life, and they still hold. However, my *container* for it all has gotten bigger and much more marvelously mysterious over the years as I've continued to awaken to Presence and the holy nature of all that is—of life, love, and beauty. At the same time, my problems with all institutionalized religions, Christianity included, have increased because their distortions and distance from their core teachings have caused, and continue to cause, most of the world's problems. Finding a spiritual unity of purpose is perhaps our biggest challenge as a species.

If asked how I have come to think of myself, I would say that I am a contemplative/poet/writer/priest/counselor/mother/grandmother/wife with an abiding curiosity about theology, ecology, quantum science, astrophysics, and archetypal, evolutionary astrology. As I keep growing in self-awareness, I would like to add that I am also, perhaps, becoming a more wise and compassionate listener/guide.

If asked what I have learned along the way that I could offer others, I would say face your pain/griefs/fears and trace them to their source for comfort and healing. Ask your soul questions and then watch and listen closely for glimpses of the guidance that will always come. And dare your deepest, most creative dreams because that is our calling as human beings. I would add that we are in a most critical period of time, but archetypes are shifting and the Spirit is afoot. So go for it and do your work!

I would also say now that quantum consciousness is the field that holds all things and all fields. Everything exists within it and partakes of it, so everything is Holy, everything is One. And I would say that we human creatures all long at some level for a more spacious experience of participation in this divine reality, this oneness. Otherwise we are, to one degree or another, lost in our little lonely selves and adrift in our conflicting worldviews. But that for which we long is always available, always inviting us to see. In fact, it is not so much something to be found as it is the very Self that is seeking! It is forever manifesting itself in the beauty and diversity all around us—from stars in the sky, to stones on the shores, to trees in the woods, to the many faces of humankind. I have some measure of hope that enough of us will *pay attention*, wake up, grow up, and learn peace so that we won't destroy ourselves altogether but instead find a way to meet at the table of life. We have a long evolutionary path to travel before that happens, but moment by moment, in the Presence of Love…well, that's a different story.

Part II

Some Stories of Our Times

Chapter 12

Experiencing the Era of Eris

There is a Chinese curse that says, "May you live in interesting times!" Cursed or not, here we are. *Interesting* is certainly one word for life in the early twenty-first century. The archetype of Eris, the goddess of chaos and discord, is an apt astrological marker for these years. There is also another. Throughout the turbulent 1960s, the conjunction (closeness from earth's viewpoint) of the planets Uranus and Pluto archetypally reflected the wild dynamics of that period. These planets have been going through the next phase of their relationship, the quarter phase, for several years now. We have been seeing the exaggerated uprising of many of the dynamics that were left unresolved after the sixties. And we are seeing similar dynamics to those of the preceding quarter phase in the 1930s with the rise of Nazism. In this century, though, Eris is an archetype that encompasses all this and calls us both to awaken to the repercussions of our greed and exclusionary practices and to evolve as a species in the century ahead. The Eris archetype is not afraid of strife or chaos. In fact, she provokes it to reveal the hidden dynamics of a situation on behalf of all who are disenfranchised. She is an archetype with enough power and patience to hold us as we seek to work together toward new and healthier ways of being on the planet.

While writing about my own story of awakenings, I gathered notes on current events, both polarizing and promising, that seemed to be signs of these shifting times. I did this to offer touchstones for consideration, knowing that these are but the tips of a few icebergs. Their huge bulks lie below the surface of global suffering. These icebergs desperately need attention, but that work is beyond the scope of this book. I don't know any more than anyone else where it is all headed or when breakthroughs might happen. I have just had these inklings of a new archetype on the move, one that I seem called to point to as a potential signpost or guide for this era. It all feels a little like the inklings I had when we conceived the circle work at Greenfire.

Sherri Mitchell makes it very clear in *Sacred Instructions* that, according to Native American traditional wisdom, we are each meant to be here, meant for and needed in these times. I have long had a similar intuition from my experience with astrology. Once I began to grasp the implications of my birth chart, I sensed its rightness, as if I knew at a deep level that this was the inner work I was here to do, the parents I was meant to have, and so forth. I felt as though I had assented to this journey before I was born. Other people whose charts I have worked with, even very difficult and challenging charts and lives, have told me the same thing: that they had somehow assented to their journey. Might this mean that my draw to Eris is part of the super-Libra work of my life? In any case, here we are, and we each have big work ahead in the ongoing struggle to discern what we might be called to offer—or, as Margaret Wheatley asks in the title to her new book, *Who Do We Choose to Be?*

We live in a time when the horror of mass shootings—even in hallowed places like schools and houses of worship—seem almost commonplace, a time when the devastating effects of climate change are undeniable, and a time when the polarizing effects of dualistic thinking—black/white, male/female, objective/subjective, the Right/ the Left, mind/heart, sinner/saint—have practically paralyzed our cultural and political processes. We are in desperate need of larger vessels to contain new visions. Throughout this book, I've frequently used lines from an early poetic piece I wrote about Eris, the uninvited goddess who showed up anyway to offer a provocative challenge: *Everyone must be invited to the party—everyone must have a seat at the table!* *Everyone* means to me people of all races, creeds, ethnicities, nationalities, sexual orientations, and abilities, however different—as well as our future descendants. Ultimately, it surely must mean all sentient beings. *A seat* means dignity, personhood, respect, freedom. And *the party* or *the table* means food, water, air, provisions, clothes, shelter, safety—the health of the very earth itself. It all needs to be addressed because, as Elizabeth Warren, United States Senator from Massachusetts, once famously said, "If you don't have a seat at the table, you're probably on the menu!"

What might this metaphor of greater inclusion at the party of life mean in practice? How could everyone be included at the table in a world so divided by race, language, culture, belief, gender identity, mental and physical ability, and so forth? After a year like 2018, for which the Oxford dictionaries selected *toxic* as the international word of the year, where would we begin? The changes needed are still unimaginable on a large scale, but as a long-term vision or goal, anything less than a sustainable provision of the basic necessities of life for everyone is morally unacceptable. So I suggest that we begin by facing the toxicity of our times realistically, even as we keep watching for signs that give us hope.

In this country, we have been living with the seeming failure of the Rev. Dr. Martin Luther King Jr.'s dream of ushering in a just and loving community, as well as President Obama's more recent vision of hope and change. We seem to be stuck, even regressing in many ways, with the current resurgence of white supremacist and nationalist views that were promulgated in previous centuries and various countries by white men fearing that their race and cultural dominance were under attack. Perhaps most well-meaning folks in the U.S. had naïvely hoped that the fulfillment of King's visions could happen without our country's repentance of its historical sins: the genocide of our indigenous peoples, the enslavement of peoples from many African nations, the incarceration into concentration camps of Japanese and Japanese-American people during World War II, the greedy plunder of our land and resources, and so much more. These collective atrocities underlie our national psyche and keep bubbling up because that which is not acknowledged festers and grows—for example, nowadays we are separating untold thousands of undocumented immigrants from their children at our borders and incarcerating them all. Instead of learning to develop community, we are intensifying division and polarization. Racism flourishes in its many subtle and not-so-subtle manifestations, and oppressors keep more and more of the spoils.

In *Sacred Instructions*, Sherri Mitchell traces the roots of such current realities to the doctrine of global colonization established in 1492 by Pope Nicholas V's *Romanus Pontifex*. It sanctified the enslavement of all conquered peoples, as well as their lands and goods, by their Christian colonizers, who were instructed to claim or consume everything in their path. In this country, the nineteenth-century social theory of Manifest Destiny similarly stated that white Christians were chosen and entitled by God to claim any land and goods they pleased throughout the Americas. There is still an underlying presumption that white Anglo-Protestant Christians are the rightful heirs of this nation's wealth and the core of its identity. Generations of Irish and other immigrants shifted that a bit to include Roman Catholics, so many tend to think of this as a *Christian nation*. The deeply Judeo-Christian notion of welcoming the stranger and helping those in need inspired this country for years to welcome *the huddled masses yearning to breathe free* from other *teeming shores*, as written on the plaque at the base of the Statue of Liberty. It is a belief that still prevails in many laws and hearts, but we are in a time of extreme backlash with violent anti-immigrant sentiments, resurgent antisemitism, and blatant racism on several fronts. And we are in a time of unparalleled global disparity between the haves and the have-nots, rendering millions in the United States and untold millions of refugees elsewhere homeless.

I have felt for a long time that it is blindingly obvious that you can't sustain a growth-based economy indefinitely on a finite planet. You can keep trying to stoke our already unbridled consumerism in an effort to maintain growth, but there are limits, and along the way many *someones* will be expendable losers. In the end, life itself will lose. Poverty abounds in a world where there is more than enough to go around if it were shared instead of hoarded. But global capitalism ensures that while things last, the profits rise and collect in a greedy pool at the top—shareholders take all—a short-term grab that leads to long-term devastation. Perhaps many of the super-wealthy recognize that resources can't last indefinitely, so they say, in effect, "I'm going to grab as much as I can for me and mine, and the heck with the rest of you."

Although the extreme poverty in many third-world countries is all too apparent, the extent of poverty in the United States is vastly under-recognized. The poor know they are unseen, but who can they blame? White people who feel marginalized seem reluctant to blame big business, despite its polluting effects, if that is the only hope of employment they see. It is easier for them to blame immigrants and those who have theoretically benefited from affirmative action rather than their fellow whites—however privileged those people are with wealth and power. As injustice and inequity increase, it serves those at the top to foster that blame, that sense of white victimhood, so their increasing selfishness is hidden and their devaluation of labor is disguised. They can say in effect to frustrated whites, "You could become like us if it weren't for those others, because *we* are all white." This lie is necessary because those at the top would be too vulnerable if the truth of their manipulations was actually seen.

Apart from a miracle, the rich and powerful will never voluntarily relinquish their power and money, never voluntarily acknowledge that the global political/military/industrial complex is unsustainable and corrupt at the core. Knowingly or not, it was designed and is maintained so that they will get more by way of others—primarily people of color—getting less. The rugged individualism and sense of entitlement that so shaped American life and the "American dream" have led us to this me-and-mine-at-the-center mentality of individual private rights and self-centered capitalism. While people can be urged to *give* or *share* more, we seem incapable of demanding that they *take less* or *change the system* that privileges them so unfairly. And they are, after all, in charge of that system. As Jimmy Carter once observed about our present-day governmental processes, "The United States is an oligarchy with unlimited political bribery."

A great many divisive factors—including the interference of Russia—played out in the election of Donald Trump as president in November 2016. It revealed the resentment and rage of many blue-collar white men—fearful of losing status as demographics continue to change, and fearful of losing pride and their way of life as traditional work continues to lose value. Many highly educated and privileged white men also voted for Trump, clearly wanting their privilege and power to stay intact. "He will be good for business," I kept hearing. In many cases, both groups were supported by their wives. It was also glaringly apparent how Trump played upon the nascent anti-Muslim sentiments that have ballooned with the excuse of terrorism, as well as the anti-immigrant sentiments that have increased with the relative stagnation of income in this country for all but elite whites. The abortion issue also played a huge role in the election—stoked by a man who has flip-flopped on the topic and a party that doesn't seem to want either easy access to birth control or basic aid for babies and unwed mothers, for poor children and their families, or even for public schools. This is devastating for those of us for whom being on the side of life clearly means being pro-choice, being pro a woman's right to have access to birth control and family health care—basically her right to have control over her own body and future.

Almost immediately following Trump's election, flyers inviting people to join the local Ku Klux Klan were distributed in two neighboring towns here in Maine. The next day, our daughter Anna, who was already upset about the flyers, was pumping gas at a local station when a guy driving by in a truck yelled out to her, "Get out of here, you nigger!" This was a first for her, in Maine or elsewhere, and the synchronicity of its timing with Trump's election was obvious. Hate had been sanctioned at the top. Anna decided that her response would be to craft a brief statement, have it made into posters and bumper stickers, and sell these at cost to anyone who wanted one. On a purple background with a white olive branch and white lettering, her statement reads, "I stand up against hate and intolerance in my community and in the world!" I still have mine on my car.

We certainly seem to have moved into a post-truth era of strife and discord, the qualities traditionally assigned to Eris. All sides battle for the spoils of ongoing wars and for space at the tables of power. Meanwhile, colonialism is still practiced by transnational companies that wrest resources from countries and peoples globally. The *lowest prices* usually reflect the *highest hidden costs* in terms of human health and culture, species survival, and the environment.

Threaded throughout and enhancing the devastating dynamics of our time is an increasing distrust of the mainstream news media, fueled by Donald Trump's never-ending accusations of "Fake news!"

While many of us have realized in recent years that wealth and power have increasingly controlled the content and style of the media, our underlying trust in the value of the free press prevailed, especially through the reporting of several respected journalists. Now it is all under assault and becoming so manipulated and divided by opposing political agendas, so bogged down with shallow dramas, that its future is at risk. Many of us verge on *outrage overload*, hardly knowing where to turn for trustworthy information.

This just complicates the already problematic overload of information globally. With the amount of data available doubling exponentially all the time, it's no wonder that people seek certainty and control; no wonder that fundamentalism—*don't bother me with your "facts" because I know I'm right*—is on the rise. Complexity, information overload, and mystery always threaten both those who feel marginalized and those intent on power and control because these things represent unknowns, and unknowns seem dangerous to the small, egoic self. It is crucial that more and more of us cultivate gradual, humble ways to stretch into diversity and mystery, to tolerate paradox and not knowing, so that our fears can quiet down and compassion can arise. We need to do our inner work and deal with our own shadow so that we don't project it out into the world. And we need to cultivate practices that increasingly center us in our deepest selves, the place where we are all one and can begin to learn how to be together at the table.

Whatever *prayer* means for any of us, it is sorely needed in these times. I, for one, loved coming across the following version of the Episcopal Prayers of the People, which was used in our little church but came originally from—of all places—Trinity Church on Wall Street in New York City:

- Pray for those who are hungry. Pray harder for all who will not feed them.
- Pray for those who struggle each week to pay their bills. Pray harder for all who do not care.
- Pray for those who are homeless. Pray harder for those who deny them shelter.
- Pray for those who cry out for dignity. Pray harder for all of us who do not listen.

- Pray for those oppressed by unjust wages. Pray harder for those who exploit them.
- Pray for us as we seek God's justice in our communities. Pray harder for our own transformation, that we may become the change we seek in the world.

So, we pray—whatever that means to us. We do our inner work. We offer our gifts to the world. And we look for signs of hope. Conflict may be inevitable in human affairs but, when addressed, can reveal the issues more fully and lead to change. Chaos creates havoc, as Margaret Wheatley notes in *Who Do You Choose to Be?* But also, in time, chaos creates information and new possibilities. That's the cause the Eris archetype most truly serves. Her so-called trouble-making at the wedding feast revealed the consequences of avaricious self-interest. Furthermore, as Wheatley says, change is always happening, but it is always surprising and usually emerges from messiness and mix-ups. The chaos and discord of these times provide an apt opportunity, then, for positive change. Perhaps Eris's archetypal connection with competition can help us see what our greedy grabbing-up of earthly goods is doing to our planet so that we can learn, instead, to use our competitive impulses for the sake of global justice and balance by creating alternative resources, meaningful work, and sustainable economies. Perhaps the implications of her myth—that everyone must be invited and included at the party of life—will, in time, take hold of our global consciousness.

As I've prepared for this book, I've noted many signs of awakening and change that have given me *hope*. These include the following:

- the 2006 film *What the Bleep Do We Know!?*, which revealed to the public the ramifications of quantum theory for our understanding of consciousness;
- The Occupy Wall Street movement, which illuminated the extreme wealth of the 1%;
- the nationwide legalization of gay marriage in 2015;
- the #MeToo movement, an international protest against sexual harassment and assault that began in 2017 with one woman's Twitter posting;

- the Women's Marches that took place around the world in 2017 and several times since;
- the 2018 student-organized March for Life protesting the NRA and subsequent such protests;
- Grannies Against the Right, a grassroots movement of older women that began in Austria and is quickly spreading in protest of far-right policies;
- the 2018 Nobel Peace Prize awarded to two people for their campaigns against the use of rape as a weapon of war;
- the work of Teaching While White, which addresses how to be consciously, intentionally, anti-racist in the classroom;
- the new National Memorial for Peace and Justice in Montgomery, Alabama, which commemorates the more than 4,400 African-American people who were lynched or otherwise murdered by mobs of white people between 1877 and 1950;
- the opening of the Smithsonian National Museum of African American History and Culture in Washington, DC;
- the increasing acceptance of certain mind-altering substances to help treat such conditions as depression, anxiety, addiction, and post-traumatic stress disorder;
- the record-setting victories for women and various minority groups in the 2018 midterm elections.

On a totally different, archetypal level, a sign of hope for me was the 2014 movie *Maleficent*, which is a new take on the "Sleeping Beauty" fairy-tale version of the Eris myth. The starring role of the uninvited fairy, Maleficent, is played by Angelina Jolie, woman-warrior actress and Eris exemplar (her birth chart has a very influential Eris placement). The terrified king in the movie brings down everything in his world just to protect himself from the supposed wrath and justice-seeking power of Maleficent. In the end, though, the movie is all about beauty, peace, and the power of love. I see it as an archetypal story of the possibility of awakening from the deep sleep of unawareness and division into greater compassion and care for the earth.

This message and the lush, imaginative imagery of Maleficent's fairy realm reminded me of the popular 2009 movie *Avatar*, which is about a highly evolved alien species on the fictional moon Pandora, who are able to link their minds and energy for healing and for combating the attempted takeover by a greedy mining corporation from Earth. Might it be that this moon's name alludes to Pandora's mythical box and Eris's daughter Hope, who remains locked in there? *Avatar* closes with a most compelling and unforgettable image of awakening.

I also delighted in the 2017 movie *Wonder Woman*. She was the only comic-book heroine of my youth, a justice-wielding icon for a generation of girls like me who were hungry for more. It was great to be reminded of her story and to see her familiar figure on the big screen these many years later. The movie opens with images of her birth community of powerful, compassionate women. Even when it shifts to the violent context of World War II, Wonder Woman remains powerfully feminine, thoughtful, and compassionate, always ready and willing to turn aside from her wartime mission in order to give immediate aid to suffering individuals.

Both Wonder Woman and warrior woman Xena of television fame were imagined as growing up in a caring, empowering community of women—Amazons—and both were trying to deal with Ares, the Greek god of war (the Roman Mars). Could it be that it is women who must face and grapple with archetypal powers of war and greed if the world is to change? It's a daunting task because we know that powerful females are almost always derided as troublemakers. But what hope they can inspire! I think of the respect and awe New Zealand's prime minister, Jacinda Arden, engendered when she donned a hijab (headscarf) in solidarity with Muslim women after the mass shootings at two Christchurch mosques in March 2019 and then, six days later, announced plans to ban semi-automatic rifles in her country.

Whatever all this might ultimately mean, we can imagine the archetype of Eris, warrior-like sister of Ares, being with us in these times. She has been in the astrological sign of Aries since the 1920s—in other words, throughout the lifetime of almost all of us. In that sign, her aggressive, troublemaking aspects would be most apparent. In 2048, however, she will move into the astrological fixed-earth sign of Taurus. By then, it might be that every issue facing humanity will *undeniably* revolve around the fate of our planet.

The 2018 movie *RBG* gave us all a heroine more than worthy of the big screen, but this time a real person. The film is an intimate and moving portrayal of Supreme Court Justice Ruth Bader Ginsburg, a woman of towering intellect, insight, and foresight, a woman not afraid of the intricately detailed, many-layered efforts necessary to bring about greater justice for all women in this country. In her eighties, she is still persevering in that work, despite health challenges and the odds against her. The film enables us all to see and hear her as the legal legend and icon of hope she truly is.

Then in 2018 came *The Black Panther* movie with its celebration of African beauty, art, and archetypes and its emphasis on the passionate pursuit of justice and peace. This widely popular film—the third-highest-grossing of all time—depicts a fictional, fundamentally just and compassionate African nation, Wakanda, which was never colonized and which has technology and resources beyond any other nation. The movie portrays many dynamic, fully empowered, women warriors, leaders, and scientists—all in gorgeous, African-inspired costuming. It offers a wide range of vision and possibilities for every one of us, but particularly for those of African descent, for women, and for young people. Today's youth so need to be liberated from their cyber-world addiction with its resulting loss of interpersonal relationships and its disconnection from their embodied selves. The explicit final message of the movie is that all nations must find a way to work together as one family on the earth.

As I write this, the world is watching the United States gear up for the crucial 2020 presidential election. There are several powerful women candidates in the race and many other women who moved into the public eye with the 2018 midterms. They all face the perennial issues of what kind of behavior, dress, and demeanor the public will tolerate from women. To survive, they will need the courage and power of their whole beings, including any parts of themselves that have been relegated to the shadows as unacceptable. In other words, they will need their anger! Black women have long been stigmatized as angry, and angry white women have long been stigmatized as *bitches* or *witches*, but isn't it long past time for *all* women to let loose their full power, including their outrage, and act from it?

While I say that women must unleash the power of our anger as we seek to act on behalf of ourselves and the planet, we must simultaneously learn to let it flow through us so we don't get bogged down in it. That necessitates probing its roots in us and finding healing. Only then can our anger be clean, just, and for the sake of all. Only then can we listen to one another and act from a place of guidance, wisdom, and love. These are ultimately the most powerful motivators. The long-hidden and feared dark feminine includes much that is golden and beautiful. It all needs to be freed so that it can be faced, sorted, and channeled for good.

We are in a struggle for global justice and well-being that seems eternal because for every few steps forward, we experience backlash and backsliding. Furthermore, it is still early in that struggle, early in understanding that everything is connected and affects everything else. I find myself wondering, without much hope at times, whether the nascent recognition of violence against women and all oppressed people might open the way for the United States to begin to acknowledge our genocide of indigenous peoples and our history of slavery, racism, and white privilege—the repercussions of which are tearing us apart to this day. Until we do so, we will not be able to see just how systemic and subtly pervasive our resentment of difference is and how easily the alt-right can be encouraged and manipulated.

As Sherri Mitchell points out in *Sacred Instructions*, any hope of real transformation must be preceded by genuine repentance for our country's history of oppression. We watched the events at Standing Rock in 2016 as thousands of native and non-native people gathered to protect the waters and ancestral burial grounds threatened by the Dakota access pipeline. Most of us were unaware of the full history of ongoing violence that underlies that story. In her book, Mitchell fills it in a bit but augments the telling with her personal, familial, and tribal story of the horrific violence and slaughter perpetrated against her own Penobscot nation in Maine. She offers readers like me, from the dominant culture, a taste of the grief and pain of the oppressed and thus awakens a taste of the consequential guilt and helplessness of the oppressor—of our tendency to back away from genuine encounters because the stories seem so shameful and the historical gap so un-crossable. We all must find ways to bridge this gap—these many gaps—between oppressed and oppressor in our country and the world. To do this work, Mitchell says, we will have to begin in small ways—person to person, community to community. We will each have to learn to bear our grief and our guilt. And we will have to deal with the backlash of those who refuse to see and to participate, be they strangers or beloved members of our own family.

In the end, though, we will each have to deal with ourselves. Although I consciously delight in difference, I know that as a white person I have to examine continually how an underlying fear of difference is still at work in me. The fact is that I have been relatively privileged by education and profession, if not so much by birth—my maternal grandfather was a custodian in the Boston public schools and a true Archie Bunker bigot. However, I have lived most of my life in fairly privileged white liberal environments. Much as I want to care, I know I cannot presume to understand the devastating sense of powerlessness and/or rage felt by those in this country and elsewhere who can't find meaningful, life-sustaining work and who see their traditional lifestyles slipping away. Nor can I really understand the experiences of those who are overlooked, displaced, violated, victimized, or murdered because of their race, class, sexuality, ethnicity—simply because they are beautifully different from the people in power over them.

It is also true that all my children live on either the lower edge of the middle class or the upper edge of the working class, in part because a couple of them have chosen service-oriented work in semi-rural Maine: Josh is a public school teacher and Amy is a clinical social worker. The other two have had trouble at times finding fair and adequate work—and they are Black! Because of Jack's and my financial struggles during our early years of ministry and marriage—when we did not earn a living wage—I know what it is like to rely solely on hand-me-down clothes for myself and my children, to wonder where money for milk and bread will come from, and to be unable to afford dinner out or a movie. Through our work over the years with many marginalized families, and through Jack's current work with homeless young people here in Knox County, Maine, I can share, to some extent at least, in the frustration so many feel at the obscene and ever-increasing financial inequity that prevails globally. Mine is a complicated story, as is everyone's, but we each just have to keep doing the work of uncovering and healing our personal history—at all levels.

As Buddhism teaches, the biases, fears, and prejudices that have been constructed in our minds can be deconstructed. They may seem solid and irrefutable. However, upon closer, more mindful examination, they reveal themselves as simply ideas or thought patterns whose roots and conclusions can be questioned, modified, and even transformed over time. This can be a painful process because real change is stressful, and stress feels painful, even when accompanying a welcome change that also feels good. Sometimes our difficult patterns are the results of suffering, abuse, or trauma, in which case healing usually requires therapeutic intervention. In any case, a community of support can be crucial to the process of change because it helps us to see a bigger picture and to *hang in there*. I think here of Alcoholics Anonymous, the quintessential example of a community that helps to sustain people on the path of painful and total transformation. It offers proven hope that new life is always a beautiful possibility.

Bottom line: We all have to do our shadow work—our grief, anger, fear, and repentance work—because *any pain that we do not transform we will surely transmit*. We have to dive into our unconscious selves to free our soul-selves for more and more conscious living. And we have to tune in to one another to find collective guidance. If it takes a village to raise a child, it takes a much larger group to evolve enough to heal the world. We don't know how many it will take before we come to that theoretical *hundredth monkey* that will tip the balance. We do know that many wise people advise that the place to begin is locally, where and how we can, whether in politics, in a profession, on a job, on a farm, in a school, in a store, in our neighborhood, at home—wherever our lives take us. The venue doesn't matter. It's the spirit of who we choose to be, what we choose to see, and how we choose to live that matters.

Chapter 13

Exploring Quantum Consciousness

At this point in the Era of Eris, we appear to be straddling global possibilities of despair and of hope, with the weight of history and current events seemingly on the side of the former. The Eris archetype has brought us face-to-face with an extreme level of chaos and discord. But might her archetype and our times also suggest another, more awakened lens, a more hopeful understanding of human consciousness with which to build our dreams of a healthy, peaceful, more inclusive world?

As I weighed these questions, a new book by Paul Levy, *The Quantum Revelation: A Radical Synthesis of Science and Spirituality*, came to my attention. Levy writes about the revelations in consciousness possible now that we have lived for almost a century with the scientific exploration and developments of quantum theory. My background knowledge, intuition, and sense of the Eris archetype told me there were clues here for further awakening and lucid dreaming-into-being a better world. Therefore, I offer this concluding chapter on quantum consciousness, which is based on Levy's provocative and inspiring book.

So, where to begin with a subject, a mystery, that is so far outside the box of ordinary human experience that reading about it is like taking a trip down Alice's rabbit hole to a strange wonderland, a metaphor used to great effect in the movie *What the Bleep Do We Know!?* The implications of quantum theory turn classical physics upside down and inside out, although we have to continue to live our daily lives as if the old physics and old notions of causality prevail, as if there really were objective, separate things and people situated somewhere in space and time.

Quantum theory understands our whole subjective human experience to be more like an ongoing collective hallucination, a dream. It demonstrates that there is no objective reality outside the observer. Rather, we live in a participatory universe that is affected by every act of observation. For example, we can observe the wave-like behavior of *quanta* (the minimum amount of any physical entity or property involved in an interaction), but if we then try to observe their speed or location, they will behave like particles and no longer like waves. As Levy points out, it is a universe in which the subatomic quanta themselves behave as if they are observing us observing them, and as if, in the process, they instantaneously synchronize with the entire universe of quanta. Furthermore, this theory has been proven beyond a doubt. No scientific theory has ever been subjected to more scrutiny, and it has stood up to every test. Almost all the developments of the past century—from atomic bombs and lasers to MRI's and all our electronic devices—are based on it. But what the *it* is remains a mystery, one that points us toward the nature of consciousness itself.

These are strange times, indeed. And the power of the science that has emerged makes them dangerous times as well. For example, we are all being confronted by huge questions about the risks versus the benefits to humanity of various uses of algorithms, genetic engineering, and artificial intelligence (AI). So we must start participating consciously and become co-dreamers of our shared dream. Physicist John Wheeler, whom Levy quotes extensively, goes so far as to suggest that it seems we are being issued an invitation from the universe itself to wake up to its true nature of quantum consciousness, an invitation to engage our creative imagination—which Jung called "the Ground of the psyche"—to reveal our own authentic magic and beauty. According to Wheeler, it's as if the light that is the nature of the universe called forth the evolution of the eye in order to be seen and experienced, or the atom called forth physicists for its nature to be explored, or that we are being called forth to become the mirrors of consciousness and co-creators of its dream. For him, it's almost as if we human beings are the tools for a curious universe to become aware of itself and to evolve.

The following poem from my previous book, *Peacework Quilt*, uses the metaphor of song but seems apropos in this context:

#33 "The Song" (slightly modified)

I would write messy
musical lines outside
the box with echoes
from beyond the pale.
I would sing off-kilter
and off-key that music
of the spheres my soul
dimly remembers
from before and after
time—I mean this time
here now which I try
to manage in my daily
round but which is cracked
by beauty asymmetrical
so that light shines through
everywhere as the whole show
every wave/particle dances
to inaudible quantum strings
of song.

In exploring quantum consciousness, we move into the archetypal arenas of imagination and dreaming, indeed into an infinite spectrum of possibilities based on the uncertainty principles of quantum physics. This includes our experience of time as well as of space. We can know the past only by observing our experience in the present, so the past is continually being rewritten or recreated by our participation and remembrances. For example, as Agnes Sanford taught, we can heal memories of past emotional wounds in the present as we reengage with them from a more enlightened self. We are dealing here with questions about the very nature and meaning of life—my questions at age twelve—and it seems that the very questions we ask make a difference. We are discovering ourselves to be the agents of evolution through the sacred power of our minds and hearts. Therefore, more and more of us need to develop the deeply spiritual capacity to hold this vision so that we can participate wisely in dreaming the world that consciousness—the Universe, the Source, the Ground-of-Being, the Creator, the Christ, Allah, God, Love—is calling into being.

John Wheeler suggests, according to Levy, that the universe is essentially an *information-processing system* in which every part is in immediate communication with every other part. The universe uses its physical expressions to communicate with the human mind— *and vice versa.* In other words, growth and awakenings in our inner selves literally register *information* throughout the field and change the universe. Similarly, Jung sees synchronicities as messages from the universe and archetypes as *informational fields of influence* that underlie and inform our experiences. Since we human beings seem to have been given the task of making meaning out of our experiences and our quantum explorations, the hold of the Eris archetype on my imagination makes total sense. In fact, it might be said that I am *channeling* her informational field. According to physicist David Bohm, author of *Wholeness and the Implicate Order* among other books, this meaning-making work is what bridges the physical and mental realms, and it is one of the major expressions of consciousness. Without it, we are lost within ourselves and within the cosmos.

So here we are in the eternal now of our observations, experiencing what seems to be a stable and classic universe, but all the while discovering that these seemingly real things can't truly be regarded as real at deeper levels of observation. A helpful analogy here, Levy suggests, is a rainbow. It doesn't exist apart from the observing eye, but it appears to be in different places to other eyes or to eyes that change locations. The universe—apparently mostly empty space—is actually an overflowing fullness of creativity, which issues forth into and out of phenomena and form. It is an inseparable and entrancing dance of mind and matter.

The boundary between the quantum and the classical *reality* is hard to pin down because, at one level, there isn't really a boundary, just as there isn't really a boundary between the conscious and the unconscious. However, we tend to use a different language and vocabulary in talking about the two. For example, in this book I have written primarily in the classic language of the familiar world of form, time, and space. I have also often discussed the quantum realm of awakenings—of magic, dreams, archetypes, and synchronicities—although I haven't labeled it as such. We may not be able to talk *directly* about the two realities at the same time, but we can appreciate the validity of each in its own way and apply our understanding accordingly. Basically, the more aware we are of the dance of complementarity between these realities, the more we can make informed choices about how we want to use the imaginative power of our minds to influence the more ordinary world of our lived experience.

Levy suggests throughout his book that enough of the strange world of twentieth-century quantum studies may have made its way into the understanding of enough twenty-first-century people that the line between physics and metaphysics is disappearing. For example, our daughter Anna has always been a bit of a psychic, has always picked up on *vibes*. Now she is using this skill as a Reiki practitioner and studying with a medical intuitive in order to develop her psychic healing abilities. This all seems fairly normal these days to most people I know. During the last century, the uses of quantum physics proliferated in countless ways, for good and for ill—for human health and well-being as well as purely for profit and power. Perhaps in this century, as the possibilities of quantum consciousness continue to spread via the collective unconscious, we can learn to influence the use of physics more creatively for good. This is no easy journey, but it is becoming ever more important.

I was appalled, though not totally surprised, to learn that using the power of the collective mind to influence reality has become an explicit tactic of the alt-right. In taking credit for Trump's victory, Richard Spencer, one of the leading voices in the alt-right movement, declared, "We willed Donald Trump into office. We made this dream our reality." The Internet can clearly now be used as a kind of *psychic ether* to transmit the willed intentions of any group who can manipulate it. The *magic* happens when something created on the *inner mind world* of the Internet bleeds into the *real world* and changes it. We can see this dynamic playing out daily as Trump functions by the seat of his pants, capturing attention like a magician and repeating his stories until they take on a kind of reality—not only for his followers, but also for those who talk, write, or read about them even when they don't believe them. The power—and therefore the public responsibility—of the media should never be under-estimated! Similarly, we can see and feel the almost tangible force field created by white supremacists globally with their speakers, rallies, and political influence, all of which makes the news big-time, according them increased heft and standing.

It is crucial that we recognize the negative forces afoot on the planet so that we don't fall prey to them, either by going numb or by becoming entranced with the dance. Instead, we need to look deeply enough into our lingering fears and issues that we can question and possibly uproot and release them. And we need to center ourselves deeply enough in our nonreactive selves that we can abide more fully in the loving energy we want to emanate and make manifest. All my life experiences have convinced me that life is relationships and that love is our birthright, our natural milieu. Love and peaceful relationships create a much more powerful force field than hate and greed. So our work, individually and corporately, is learning to abide in and cooperate with this force field of love and peace—in ourselves, our families, and our neighborhoods to begin with, and then on into our communities and the world. Quantum consciousness informs us that this kind of force field is both real and powerful. In fact, it is the deepest and truest reality. And it is on our side—on the side of beauty, creativity, and the healthy evolution of life. It is like a teacher who has come because our species is ready to wake up to its lessons and receive its unfolding guidance. Levy says this is an *evolutionary imperative* that we dare not ignore.

As physics and psyche are increasingly seen as two complementary sides of the same coin, we need to learn to hold their seeming contradictions without fear so we can work with them more meaningfully and appropriately. The great paradox is that we are both distinct individuals *and* members of the collective web of relationships in our communities, our country, and our world. Similarly, we need *both* to be *grounded in our own physical health* and to become *more at home in the world of the collective imagination.*

Physicists are in dialogue with the Dalai Lama in an effort to further understand the nature of consciousness, while Jungian and other depth psychologies, as well as the world's mystical and indigenous traditions, offer contributions. It seems that it is time for us to adopt the "beginner's mind" of Buddhist practices and enter anew into the exploration of our own consciousness, individually and collectively. We are more mystics than we let ourselves know. We all have moments of awe and awakening, of being touched by something wonderful and lifted out of our ordinary lives, however briefly. This is the path to becoming the person we already truly are.

As mystics and meditators on the contemplative journey discover, the mirage of the separate self appears more and more as the delusion it is in quantum reality. As that veil is lifted, the sense of oneness, of the Now, appears ever more true and meaningful. This self-transcendent perspective changes everything, making the world enchanting and leading us closer to what has been called the soul. Seeing one another through this lens as sacred and blessed is possible only to the extent that we no longer simplistically see ourselves as separate beings but are increasingly able to see ourselves as an expression of the whole.

Part of our human task, according to Levy, is to celebrate the inventive work of poets and writers and to create a new and more symbolic language with which to talk about our dreams for the world, because language and thought reflect each other. Many of our current forms of communication are rooted in the classic understanding of reality and therefore hold us in that old spell. Since we now know the underlying nature of the universe involves consciousness, we can celebrate the power of our minds to think new thoughts, dream new dreams, and discover more life-sustaining ways to live on our planet. I trust that speaking in this book about archetypes, synchronicities, spirit, magic, hope, and awakenings is a step in the right direction.

We have choices to make. I think of the passage from Deuteronomy 30:19: "Behold, I have set before you life and death, blessing and curse; therefore choose life, that you and your descendants may live." In this era, it is clear that what is at stake is the life and health of our children and our children's children—indeed, of our forests, oceans, air, water, and the very earth itself. The choices we make depend a lot on our language and symbols, which are the connectors between our inner and outer worlds. New symbols—or new understandings of old symbols—open new doors to fresh possibilities of experience. When we create new images, they become part of the quantum field of information and open the way for new patterns and new behaviors to emerge. In this way, we serve as vehicles or channels for the manifestation of quantum creativity. As we cultivate loving awareness and openness to the underlying consciousness from which everything arises, we can trust that what is needed will arise—that we are actually conduits for the evolution of consciousness.

This all seems particularly significant to me because the vision and purpose of this whole book is essentially to offer the Eris archetype as a potentially informative and encouraging symbol of awakening for this new era, the twenty-first century. Another form of the provocative Eris myth of the uninvited goddess is the "Sleeping Beauty" fairy tale. Levy notes that the great scientist Erwin Schrodinger, in his book *Science and Humanism*, uses this fairy tale with its spell of sleep—cast by the uninvited fairy godmother over the land—to address the problems confronting modern physics. How, Schrodinger asks, is humankind to *awaken* from the old paradigms that enforce the separation of subject/object, you/me?

In the remnants that have survived of the ancient Eris myth, we find no story of awakening, just stories of her daring confrontation with the power structures of her day, of the revelatory results of her action, of her ability to help stop the sun, of her connection with healthy competition, and of her troublesome daughters released from Pandora's box while her daughter Hope remains imprisoned. However, in the fairy-tale version and in the movie *Maleficent*, the spell of sleep is broken by true love's kiss. It is given in the case of the former by a prince but in the case of the latter by Maleficent herself, who has been restored to her real self by love, compassion, and her own strength. Her ensuing world-healing, beauty-making power is a mythical foretaste of what the Eris archetype might portend. We have yet to see the fullness of who and what she and we can be.

The release of Eris's troublesome children from Pandora's box offered an ancient mythical explanation for all human suffering. The synchronistic connection of her planet's discovery with that of dark energy suggests Eris's association with the dark feminine, with all that we fear and avoid, which makes her an archetypal force for these times. I would also suggest that, as the *mother* of these troublesome daughters, Eris represents the capacity to hold them and the sufferings they loosed with *motherly love and compassion*. We *need* such an archetypal image of enduring love in the face of suffering because, as writer/activist/Trappist monk Thomas Merton taught, we desperately need to cultivate the capacity to bear the sufferings of the world with compassion. Only then can we set the loving intention that our actions be for the good of everyone and not for our own desired outcomes. Only then can we dream a more hope-filled future and symbolically release Eris's last daughter from the box!

If we are indeed in a new era and called to dream a new world of justice and peace, a world in which *everyone*—one hundred percent of us, not just ninety-nine percent or fewer—has a place at the table, we will need the full participation of people who have been impoverished, displaced, or discriminated against—people who have been relegated to the margins for one reason or another. They see things the more privileged among us cannot see, so they have much to teach us. We will also need those of us who have been blinded by privilege to pay attention to the rest. In other words, we will need every bit of creative imagination and mutual cooperation humanly—and quantumly—possible. If we are to make healthy changes in our systems, we will need to choose thoughtful, listening leaders who offer constructive plans instead of empty platitudes, and who inspire hope instead of feeding fear. If we are to become Wheatley's *warriors for the human spirit*, we will need to find and celebrate heroines, heroes, and common folks who are nonviolent and peaceful warriors, champions of the underdog, and teachers of compassion and cooperation.

Our times require a deepening and maturing of consciousness. Only a contemplative spirituality, an expression of quantum consciousness, can transform and unify us as *one body* here on our troubled planet. It doesn't really matter what first draws us to such practices as meditation, prayer, inner reflection, service, or the cultivation of compassion. Nor does it matter what form best suits us. Contemplative spirituality in any tradition always comes to and confirms the same truth: We are all *One*. In the words of the Dalai Lama, "All people same!" We all must be included at the table because we are all inextricably linked with the fate of one another and of the earth.

We need this kind of spirituality in order to face and befriend the impermanence of life and the uncertainty of these times with insight and compassion for ourselves and others. And we need it in order to discern the *middle way* between fight and flight. In the process, we will have to face our own shadows and recognize that whatever we fight or fear *out there* is also *in here, in me*—a recognition that is an essential route to true compassion. It is a difficult, humbling route, but necessary because, as Einstein so wisely said, "No problem can be solved from the same level of consciousness that created it."

Thankfully, many human beings seem to be moving into an understanding of the energetic fields in which all consciousness exists, an understanding which invites contemplation and its resultant awakenings to oneness, beauty, and concern for the earth. We may thus be maturing a bit more as a species. This won't be easy or fast, because evolution is so slow as to be virtually indiscernible on the human scale. But we do have the intuitive capacity to sense the big shifts and to consider new patterns and possibilities. And we have our imagination. We can each choose to tune in to and share the hopeful, loving images that move us so that they can be fine-tuned and crafted for the good of all.

As we participate more consciously in the evolutionary process of our species, we will find ourselves dealing with our fears—both seeing the things we do to distract ourselves from them and finding the courage to make loving and just choices in spite of them. In this way, we will open ourselves more and more to those whom we think of as different from ourselves. As we are able to meditate from our hearts on seeing and hearing the cries and visions of one another and of the planet, we will gradually learn to bear the pain around us so we can all be at the table together. As we touch deep down in our souls and remember we are all one, we will come to recognize every human being as a sister and a brother, every creature as a sacred gift, and Mother Earth as our greatest treasure whom we are called to honor and tend. As we meditate, pray, and work together, we will access the larger mind of Consciousness so that wisdom to create healing communities can emerge and be shared. Then we can learn to live mindfully, gratefully, communally, in an ever-present moment of peace.

Epilogue

Among my many roles, I've been a wife, parent, student, teacher, counselor, poet/writer, priest, and spiritual guide. As a worker with words, in whatever form, my goal in this book has been to tell the truth of my life and awakenings and the truth of what I see going on around us as honestly as I can. I am aware, though, that this has all been told through my personal lens and those of the people whose thoughts I've come across and felt led to share. I don't know, of course, who the audience for this book will be. It may be primarily white, middle-class people like myself. Much as I would like to write a book that would help wake up the world, each of us can only begin where we are with whatever insights and truths we have to offer. This is my offering.

The reality is that the unique visions and truths of each and every one of us are needed. This provocative Era of Eris invites us on a collaborative journey. We each need to take our place at the table and offer our small part in the global effort of awakening, of transformation, so that together we can serve the adventure of life, expand our consciousness, and participate in the creative work of the cosmos. The journey itself will be the joy—and well worth the pain. It will not be about arriving, but about *being in the process* of living into our deepest visions of connection, justice, and holiness in the ordinary beauty of life.

Please come join me.

Namaste,

Judith Perry Carpenter

Appendix A: Author's Astrological Chart

Natal Chart
Wednesday, October 7, 1942
15:50:00 PM EWT
Medford, Massachusetts
42N25 / 71W06
4:50:00 PM GMT
Tropical Placidus True Node

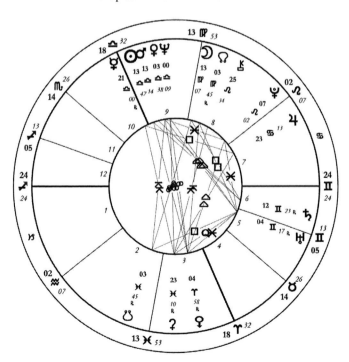

Appendix B: The Enneagram

The Enneagram is a tool with ancient roots that came into popularity in this country late in the last century, initially through the Jesuits. The word means *the graph of nine* and refers to nine basic personality fixations, which are numbered and placed around a circle diagram with lines between the types indicating directions of integration and dis-integration. The circle and lines illustrate the fluidity and complexity of the system. There are no boxes. Three of the nine are head or fear types (who, in essence, are wondering, "What's going on here?"); three are heart or image types (who, in effect, are asking others, "How am I doing?"); and three are gut types (who basically want to know, "Am I safe?"). The nine types correspond to the seven deadly sins plus fear and deceit.

The theory is that we each fall someplace on the circle and thus into one of the types, with influential ties to its neighboring types. Each type idealizes one aspect of personality and, over time, becomes more and more habituated to its patterns or compulsions and blind to its consequences. Once you have successfully identified your Enneagram type, you have a lifelong tool for spotting your core issues and thus freeing your richest gifts as that type. Since each type has habitually focused its attention on particular areas and issues, it has specialized perspectives to offer when less compulsively driven.

The difficulty lies in correctly identifying your type because, until you do, the tool is just an interesting and somewhat complex theory—not at all transformative. There are many quickie online tests to help people find their type, but after working with the Enneagram for thirty or more years now, including co-leading many workshops on it, I don't have much faith in those tests. The surest way to find your type is to go to a workshop with panels of participants from each of the types who reveal their issues and their stories. At some point, for most people, the penny drops and they recognize their own inner dynamics. For some, though, reading or group work with a person who is gifted at it can help.

To make this clearer, I'll say something about myself. I am a Five on the Enneagram, the head type who overdoes the thinking bit and is relatively out of touch with the body's feelings and needs. Fives are typically withdrawn individuals because they identify with being the detached, outside observer. They idealize being intelligent and pursue specialized areas of knowledge or expertise as a means of calming their fears and coping with the world. Their sin is avarice or tightness and stinginess. They hoard their own time and energy, easily feeling invaded and depleted, fearfully locked into the scarcity mode. Some also hoard books or another category of things. When disintegrating, Fives move to Seven, the head type that under-does thinking, and they get agitated and distracted. When integrating, they become more like the Eight, the gut type that can exemplify embodiment, strength, and leadership.

That I was a Five was obvious fairly quickly to me. However, it took deep work, personally and in community, for me to wake up to the price I paid for my idealizations as this type. I not only shared its core coping method of acquiring head-knowledge, but was paralyzed and withdrawn because of my pervasive sense of inadequacy (there must be something missing in me if my own mother can't see my passionate feelings) and my fear of being put on a pedestal for what I knew. It took years for me to more fully inhabit my own body, strength, and gut-knowing. And it has taken additional years for me to move from the fear of scarcity to a trust in abundance, to move from our culture's ethos of greedy consumption to the recognition that the earth could provide enough to go around if we would adopt sustainable and just practices, if we would cooperate globally for the well-being of all. This is a far-distant dream, of course, but look what the alternative is doing to us!

Scientifically, so much more is known now about neurology and the fact that *neurons that fire together, wire together,* which explains the formation and persistence of habits. It takes a long time to rewire our oldest habits, our entrenched ego identities. But we can't even begin the work until we see them and understand their repercussions in our life. I, for example, had to see how my over-done thinking was interwoven with the underlying sense of inadequacy, constriction, and energetic drain I had always felt emotionally and interpersonally. Now I can usually spot the moment when I start withdrawing and feeling tight in a situation, the point at which I start checking out the time and wondering when I can get away to replenish myself. Admitting all this is embarrassing, but it's so liberating to know that I don't need to be a victim or prisoner of these habits. I can reclaim my own power of choice and re-inhabit my own body. I can take a few deep breaths, re-center myself, and relax into the present moment and the company of the people around me with grace and gratitude. I may not always do so, but *I have the choice!* I don't know any tool that more specifically or better enables us to unmask and wrestle with conditioning at the deepest levels of psyche and spirit than the Enneagram.

Appendix C: Author's Daily Office

Before arising, I give thanks for rest and a cozy bed. Then I offer the day—its events, planned or unplanned, and the people I will encounter—to the service of love and awakening consciousness.

Later, as I center into heart prayer for others and the planet, I affirm my deepest intentions: offer gratitude and serve life, trusting guidance and abiding openheartedly in the spacious flow of grace... whatever comes...

At lunchtime, I give thanks for the blessing of food and abundance in my life. I pray for peace, for all those in need, and for greater awareness regarding my own consumption of Earth's resources.

Midafternoon, I pause to offer gratitude for the rhythm of the day and the beautiful people in my life. Savoring the sights and sounds around me, I center again into grace and peace.

Before dinner, I offer gratitude for sustenance and remember my commitment to care for my body as a holy vessel in all that I do this evening.

At bedtime, I offer gratitude for the events and encounters of the day, including lapses in love and in faithfulness to my path. I release all to Spirit, breathe deeply, and settle down to sleep.

Awakening in the night, I give thanks for sleep and the comforts of my bed. If a dream or concern is in my awareness, I consider its meaning and then let it go, breathing into my heart and relaxing back into sleep.

Bibliography

Bohm, David. *Wholeness and the Implicate Order.* Great Britain: Routledge, 1980.

Bolen, Jean Shinoda. *The Millionth Circle: How to Change Ourselves and the World: The Essential Guide to Women's Circles.* York Beach, ME: Conari Press, 1999.

Buber, Martin. *I and Thou.* New York: Charles Scribner's Sons, 1958.

Carpenter, Judith. *Peacework Quilt: 365 Meditative Offerings.* Rockland, ME: Seafire Press, 2009.

Cain, Susan. *Quiet: The Power of Introverts in a World That Can't Stop Talking.* New York: Crown Publishers, 2012.

Douglas, Lloyd C. *The Robe.* New York: Houghton Mifflin Harcourt Publishing Company, 1942.

Eisler, Riane. *The Chalice and the Blade: Our History, Our Future.* San Francisco: HarperCollins Publishers, 1987.

Episcopal Church. *The Book of Common Prayer and Administration of the Sacraments and Other Rites and Ceremonies of the Church: Together with the Psalter or Psalms of David According to the Use of the Episcopal Church.* New York: Seabury Press, 1979.

Fox, Matthew. *Original Blessing: A Primer in Creation Spirituality.* Sante Fe, NM: Bear & Company, 1983.

Gilbert, Elizabeth. *Big Magic: Creative Living Beyond Fear.* New York: Riverhead Books, 2015.

Gilligan, Carol. *In a Different Voice: Psychological Theory and Women's Development.* Boston: Harvard University Press, 1982.

Hillesum, Etty. *An Interrupted Life: The Diaries of Etty Hillesum, 1941–1943.* New York: Pantheon Books, 1983.

Howell, Alice O. *The Heavens Declare: Astrological Ages and the Evolution of Consciousness.* Wheaton, IL: Quest Books, 1990.

Jordan, Clarence. *Cotton Patch Version, 4 Volumes.* Macon, GA: Smyth & Helwys Publishing, 1968-1973.

Kornfield, Jack. *After the Ecstasy, the Laundry: How the Heart Grows Wise on the Spiritual Path.* New York: Bantam Books, 2000.

Kotler, Steven, and Jamie Wheal. *Stealing Fire: How Silicon Valley, the Navy SEALS, and Maverick Scientists Are Revolutionizing the Way We Live and Work.* New York: HarperCollins Publishers, 2017.

Lang, Andrew, ed. *The Blue Fairy Book.* Boston: Charles E. Brown and Company, 1889.

Le Grice, Keiron. *Discovering Eris: The Symbolism and Significance of a New Planetary Archetype.* Edinburgh, Scotland: Floris Books, 2012.

Levy, Paul. *The Quantum Revelation: A Radical Synthesis of Science and Spirituality.* New York: SelectBooks Inc., 2018.

Mitchell, Sherri. *Sacred Instructions: Indigenous Wisdom for Living Spirit-Based Change.* Berkeley, CA: North Atlantic Books, 2018.

Norris, Kathleen. *Dakota: A Spiritual Geography.* Boston: Houghton Mifflin Company, 1993.

Sanford, Agnes. *The Healing Light.* St. Paul, MN: Macalester Park Publishing, 1947.

Schrodinger, Erwin. *Science and Humanism.* Cambridge, MA: Cambridge University Press, 1951.

Seltzer, Henry. *The Tenth Planet: Revelations from the Astrological Eris.* Bournemouth, UK: The Wessex Astrologer Ltd, 2015.

Wheatley, Margaret J. *Who Do We Choose to Be? Facing Reality, Claiming Leadership, Restoring Sanity.* Oakland, CA: Barrett-Koehler Publishers, 2017.

Wheatley, Margaret J., and Myron Kellner-Rogers. *A Simpler Way.* San Francisco: Berrett-Koehler Publishers, 1996.

Acknowledgments

Since this book encompasses my whole life story, every person I have ever met, read, studied under, worked with, lived near, am related to, or served has impacted me in small or large ways. Many are already mentioned or alluded to in my story, and I am grateful for them all.

I specifically want to bless and thank my reader/editors Ellen Goldsmith, Janet Shea, Adelaide Winstead; initial copyeditor Susan Vaughan; and fabulous writing coach Annie Tucker. And I want to thank Jane Karker, who came up with the title for this book; Jenn Dean my project coordinator; and the rest of the staff at Maine Authors Publishing & Cooperative, who brought the book to completion. Special thanks go to Arifa Boehler, Elizabeth Garber, Shane Snowdon, and David Mumford who each reviewed the book and gave me the great gift of writing a blurb for the cover.

I also want to express my deepest gratitude for dear friends and generous benefactors of the whole process Nancy Werth, Su and Jay Murdock, and Barb and Dan Reidy. And I am grateful for the three writers whose valuable insights in their recent books I have repeatedly cited and credited throughout my book: Paul Levy for *The Quantum Revelation*, Sherri Mitchell for *Sacred Instructions*, and Margaret J. Wheatley for *Who Do We Choose to Be?* Finally, special mention is needed for my beloved husband, Jack, who encouraged and supported me every step of the way, even when I became quite obsessed with the writing and was barely present to him.

There is simply no way to try to identify all those others who made a significant contribution to my life and this book without risking the omission of equally important people. Instead, I choose to trust that you know who you are and how grateful I am that you have been in my life.

About the Author

Judith Perry Carpenter is an Episcopal priest with a Doctor of Ministry degree in Feminist Liberation Theology and Ministry from the Episcopal Divinity School in Cambridge, Massachusetts. Following earlier work in youth ministry, she served twelve years as chaplain at Dana Hall, a boarding school for girls from around the world located in Wellesley, Massachusetts. She then moved to Tenants Harbor, Maine, as one of the founders of Greenfire, a women's retreat house. For fifteen years, her Greenfire ministry involved participating in deep personal and spiritual conversations with people, primarily women, from any faith tradition or none and from many other countries. Judith is the author of *Peacework Quilt: 365 Meditative Offerings*, which was published in 2009. Currently living in Rockland, Maine, near three of her four children and her five granddaughters, Judith seeks to balance family life, the contemplative path, and a shared ministry of encouragement to youth workers with her husband, Jack.